The Weaver And The Throwster

By David Possee

The 19th Century Essex & Suffolk Silk Industry

Cover Design: © Karen Cater
Hedingham Fair, Sunnyside,
Southey Green, Hedingham, Essex CO9 3RN

Photographs by courtesy of: Braintree District Museum
Courtaulds Ltd

Printed by: PressXpress
Fox Meadow, 23 Courtauld Road,
Braintree, Essex CM7 9BD

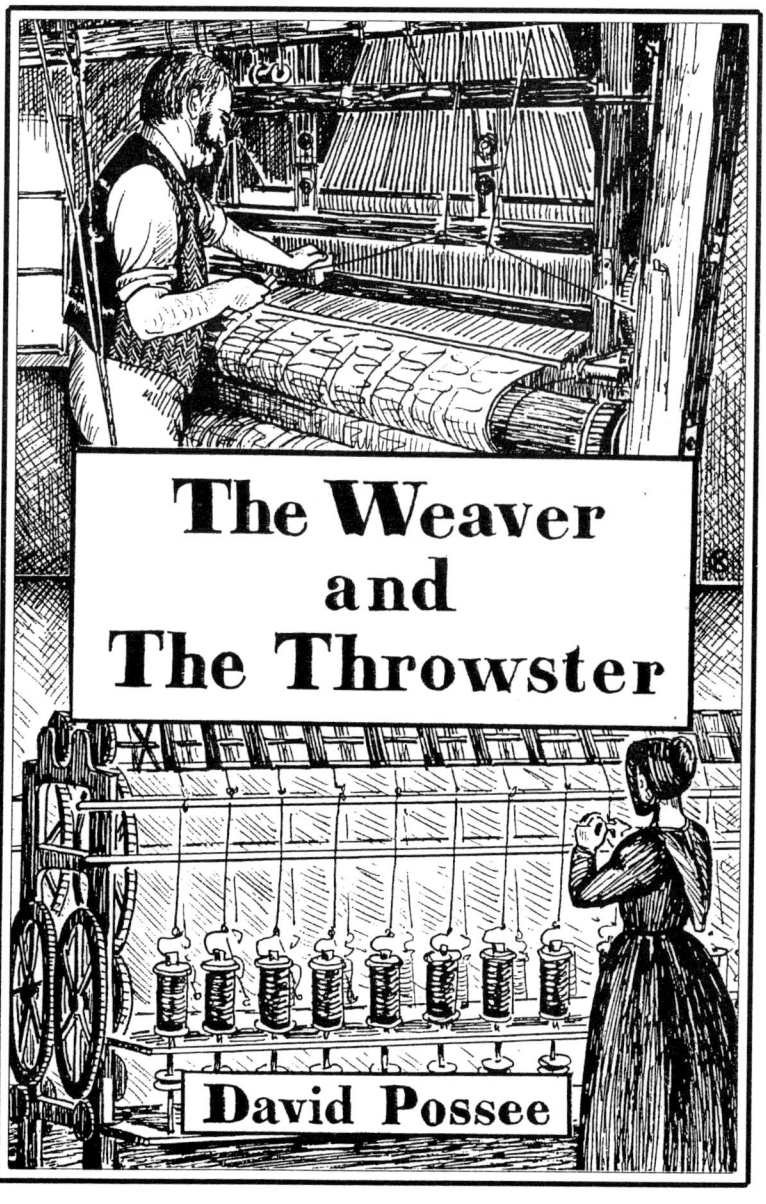

The Weaver
and
The Throwster

David Possee

Contents

The 19th Century Silk Industry of Essex & Suffolk

The silk industry played an important role in the economics of both counties throughout the 19th century and into the 20th Century as well, until its demise, particularly in Essex from the 1970's. Currently in business are The Humphries Weaving Co at Braintree and Castle Hedingham, Vanners Silk Weavers, Stephen Walters & Sons Ltd and The Gainsborough Silk Weaving Co Ltd in Sudbury. Sudbury is now considered to be the silk centre of the country.

It was an industry peppered by success and failure, boom and depression, reaching its zenith in the 1850's. A single trade agreement in 1860 caused the industry to decline rapidly and by the end of the 19th century only a handful of manufacturers were still in business.

The origins of this book lie with an essay about the 19th century Silk Industry in North Essex researched and written by the author for the Local History Certificate Course at Essex University. During the course of these researches it soon became apparent that the industry was important not only to Essex but also to Suffolk in an area some 20 miles north and south of the River Stour and well worth further research.

Whilst there are articles in existence the whole subject has not, as far as I know, been brought together recently and in this book I have tried to re-address this situation.

Because of the nature of the trade many firms left little trace of their existence either in buildings or records and so much of the evidence has had to be taken from other sources such as Census Returns, Newspapers and Trade Directories. Wherever possible I have tried to get accurate dates for the existence of the various manufacturers, but in some cases I have had to make assumptions based on the best information to hand.

I am grateful for the assistance given by both the Essex and Suffolk Record Offices. Also Richard Shackle and Patrick Crouch of the Colchester and Haverhill Local History Centres respectively, Andrew Phillips of Colchester and John Sayers of Sudbury plus local history groups and individuals who have allowed me access to their own researches.

David Possee January 1998

Chapter One

The Wool And Silk Industries

The 19th Century silk industry cannot be looked at in isolation and it must be viewed in context with the textile industry of East Anglia, going back to the 11th Century.

The art of weaving cloth goes back to the days before recorded history when our ancestors wove cloth on primitive looms for their clothes. Probably up until the 11th Century it remained predominantly a domestic craft, but from the 12th Century onwards there is a woollen cloth industry developing to supply not only people outside the local area but in Europe as well. Over the years weavers from the Continent, particularly Holland, came to England and the cloth trade developed and became an important factor in the local economy. Important centres grew up at Lavenham, Long Melford, Coggeshall, Braintree, Bocking, Dedham, Kersey and Colchester.

Research has shown that in 1750 that there were about 8000 weavers in Essex and Suffolk supported by about 55000 spinners, the majority of whom were women. It was a cottage industry with the raw materials passed on from one processor to the next, under the control of the Clothier.

Never a very stable industry it probably reached its peak in the late 17th and early 18th century. However, with the advent of the French Wars at the end of the 18th century, the market for English cloth diminished greatly, particularly when, owing to the war, the Lisbon market was no longer open. Gradually the work given out lessened and many weavers and spinners were put out of work. The records of the Overseers give a fair indication of the economic hardships brought on by the quite sudden demise of the industry.

In the North of England the woollen industry turned to other products, but in East Anglia the merchants got out of the industry altogether. Some went into farming, banking and other commercial ventures instead whilst the less fortunate found themselves bankrupted.

By the end of the 18th Century the woollen industry in Essex and Suffolk had virtually disappeared. Those who had worked in the industry found themselves out of work with no prospect of other employment as very few could afford to move to find work elsewhere, although there were opportunities owing to the French Wars of joining the Army or Navy.

Silk

The silk industry did not suddenly appear on the scene in the 19th century, as it had been part of the textile industry in England since the 15th century. The use of silk is first mentioned in the 14th century when it was being used for embroidery and for making threads, cords and braids coming into the country by merchants from Genoa in Italy. When silk weaving actually started in this country is hard to determine but mention is made in a Statute of 1455 of *"Silk women and Spinsters of Silk within the City of London ."* [1]

There is also a reference to the fact that cloth of gold, silver, and silk were being woven in London in 1473. About the same time in Norwich wool and silk were being woven together.[2] Paintings from this period onwards show their subjects wearing silk dresses, waistcoats, coats, stockings and ceremonial robes.

The wearing of silk became a mark of a person's station in society and statutes known as Sumptuary Law were passed, which prescribed the classes of people allowed to wear silk apparel. To quote from one such law from the 16th century *"forbad any man under the degree (status) of a Knight's eldest son to wear a velvet jerkin, doublet or hose, or to use satin, damask, taffeta or grossgrain (types of material) for cloaks, coats, gowns, or other uppermost garments. No woman below the degree of a Knight's wife to wear velvet or silk embroidery or netherstocks of silk ".* [3] Later on the laws were modified and by the start of the Stuart period there was a general non-observance. Irrespective of this, silk and velvet products have always commanded high prices, and in the end whether you wore silk was determined by the ability to pay the price.

Silk later became fashionable as a wall covering, and examples can be seen in most stately homes the length and breadth of the land, woven normally 21 inches wide, which accounts for the width of wallpaper as this was first produced in this country by silk fabric manufacturers such as Sanderson & Co.

1   33 Henry VI . Cap v
2   Notes on Silk Industry - J Corley
3   English Yeoman - Campbell p 253

Chapter Two
The Silk Industry And Spitalfields

Traditionally, in English towns, allied trades lived and worked in one area. The interdependence on each other was perhaps one reason for this, but also when one family moved to a town and established themselves, others from the same area would link themselves to people they already knew and where they could find a home. As far as the silk industry in London was concerned it was to the small village on the outskirts of the city called Spitalfields that the weavers and spinners were drawn. Sometime during the 16th Century many London weavers stopped weaving linen and woollen fabrics and turned to silk and this new impetus made London, and in particular the region of Spitalfields the centre of English silk weaving.

Events on the Continent, particularly France, played an important part in establishing the Silk Industry in Spitalfields. In Oct 1685 the Edict of Nantes, which gave rights to Protestants in France, was revoked. Increasingly the Protestant communities were under threat of losing their homes, trade and lives and between 200,000 and 250,000 people left France. It is reckoned that up to 1690, 80,000 settled in England, of which 25,000 came to London to live in Bishopsgate, Spitalfields, Shoreditch, Southwark, Cripplegate and Soho. Quite a number took up residence in the new houses constructed after the Great Fire of London.

The majority of those settling in the area of Spitalfields were weavers, and within 10 years there was a tenfold increase in the production of silk products. As time went on the industry became very competitive, especially from the water-powered mills in Derbyshire and as a result wages in Spitalfields were kept very low. The workers invoked the time honoured method of asking the Magistrates to fix labour rates, and the result was a Parliamentary Bill called the Spitalfields Act 1773, which fixed the payment terms of the workers, within a 3 mile radius.

The effect of this Bill was eventually to bring about much unemployment as the Merchant Weavers sought to place their work elsewhere, where rates of pay could be much lower. This brought about the movement of work into East Anglia, where, as a result of the decline of the broadcloth industry, there were people in the trade who were available for work. The Merchants found that they were able to get the work done here for two-thirds of the cost in Spitalfields. Home workers were also employed in East Ham and Stratford which were conveniently just outside the 3 mile zone.

The importance of a London address is shown by the fact that although in due course most of the production moved elsewhere, the firms always quoted their

London address in the Trade Directories and letterheads.

Textile production by the 18th century was beginning to be done in workshops, which in the first place were converted barns, houses, warehouses or corn mills. Where these were not available purpose built workshops or factories were built instead. The earliest purpose built power driven factory was a three storey silk mill built in 1702 by Thomas Cotchett in Derby.[1] With the advent of power driven factories and mills, by the end of the 18th Century other centres of weaving were being developed. In the latter half of the 18th century the French, who had always produced good quality silk, regained their traditional markets as well and both these factors had a marked affect on the London weaving community. There was also reluctance by the Spitalfield weavers to use new developments such as the flying shuttle which would have made them more productive. There is also mention made in some reports on the English silk industry that in many cases somewhat shoddy fabrics were being woven. An effort was made by the Government in 1766 to assist the home industry with a prohibition on the import of foreign silks. This legislation was replaced in 1826 by a 30% tariff being applied to silk imports, which was later reduced to 15% and removed altogether in 1860. The 1820's saw a slump in trade across the country as in common with all trades the affects of economic depression took hold. By 1830 the export of silk goods showed a marked increase. This increased production was in the main being taken on by manufacturers in the North West of England, the Midlands and the West Country, who, unlike their counterparts in Spitalfields, were using new technology such as the power loom to increase their output. The result of this competition caused large-scale unemployment in Spitalfields compounded by the movement of work out to the provinces. For instance a master silk manufacturer, Newberry, who had 200 looms at work in 1824 had only 12 by 1838, as the rest of the work was being done on power looms in Exeter.[2]

1   Building Firsts (D Crawford 1990)
2   The History of the Weavers Company

Chapter Three

Movement Into Essex And Suffolk

Mention has already been made of the competition being faced by the Spitalfields silk manufacturers. Throughout the 18th century and into the early years of the 19th this competition caused the Spitalfield merchants to look elsewhere to produce their product in order that they could compete with the much more mechanised industry in and around Derby. The first process to be moved out was that of "throwing ", which had been mechanised in 1718 and could easily be done by using water power to drive the machinery.

The result of this was that during the 18th century throwing mills were established near the Herts /Essex border. As early as 1720 mention is made of silk throwing mills in Little Hallingbury,[1] near Bishop's Stortford and it is thought that the one(s) at Sewardstone near Waltham Abbey could have been started at the same time. The Little Hallingbury mill reverted back to a corn mill and does not seem to have been operating as a throwing mill at the start of our period. Morant writing of the silk mill in his History states - *A mill here has been for many years employed in twisting and winding silk using an engine invented by William Aldersey - apprentice to a silk throwster in London for which the proprietors have a patent. The work employs a great number of women and girls in the neighbourhood.*

Ogbourne writing in 1820 about the Sewardstone mill stated that it belonged to Carr & Dobson of Cheapside. [2] In 1826 John Carr owned the mill and then from 1832 by John Buttress and subsequently J J Buttress & Son. Sometime in the 1840's it ceased as a throwing mill, but the premises continued in the silk trade as a dye house until about 1885.

At Waltham Abbey there were another 2 throwing mills, one belonging to John Woolrich and the other to Forsyth & Lincoln, but both of these were closed in the 1850's.

The first major move to North Essex took place in 1798/9 when Witts & Co purchased a watermill at Pebmarsh to be converted for use as a Silk Throwing Mill. About the same time William Newman opened a factory in Bocking in Bocking End or Rayne Road. A row of weaver's cottages are still to be found on the Bocking side of Rayne Road and these may well have been in operation at this time. In 1807 it is recorded in an unofficial census taken by the Dean of Bocking that the silk industry was well established in the town (Bocking) and that Newman had 10 employees. The factory was destroyed by fire in 1815 and little else is known of the exact site or of William Newman himself. [3]

Joseph Wilson trading as Remington, Wilson & Co moved into Megs Mill,

Chapel Hill, Braintree in 1810 and George and Samuel Courtauld were employed to convert the mill for silk winding and throwing. Samuel Courtauld set up his mill in 1816 in Panfield Lane, Braintree.

The Overseers in Glemsford put an advert in the London papers offering a site for anyone interested in building a Throwing Mill who would in the first instance, give work to the inmates of the local workhouse. The offer was taken up by Alexander Duff of Duff and Brooks who had premises at 31 Spital Square, London and the mill was opened for business in 1824.

By the end of the 1820's silk manufacturers were well established in Essex and Suffolk and the tables in appendix 1 at the back of the book give an idea of the eventual development of the industry in the two counties.

In the first instance it was silk throwing mills that were set up. The yarn was supplied from Spitalfields. Later on weaving and other processes were introduced locally as well.

Looking at the map on page 8 it can be seen that there were definite localities to which the trade was attracted. What factors determined the geographical spread?

Water: In the first instance it was the availability of power to drive the Throwing Mills. The main centres are to be found in places which had easy access to a river and water power. The rivers, Blackwater, Brain, Colne, Stour and tributaries of those rivers - the Peb and Robinsbrook provided sufficient water. All of them already supported many corn and fulling mills and some of these mills were purchased and converted for silk throwing.

Land: Secondly, there was a supply of land on which to build the silk mills and the fact that this was an area with textile experience.

Labour: The mills employed women and children to a great extent and there was this pool of labour stemming from the spinners who had worked in the now defunct woollen industry. Also Overseers were only too pleased to supply the owners with workers from the ranks of inmates of the workhouses. Some employers had employees from workhouses in London, which is borne out from details contained in the 1841 census returns, as well the Courtauld archives and letters. Such employees lived in houses built by their employers for that purpose.

Low Wage Rates: Fourthly, because of the type of labour force (mainly women and children), wage rates could be minimal, which enabled work to be done at $^2/_3$ the cost of having it done in Spitalfields.

Finally, it only took one of Spitalfields merchants to move into the two counties for his counterparts to follow suit.

Transport Costs: As work was carried out locally the cost of transporting raw materials and cloth was reduced.

Just what effect did the movement of the industry into Essex and Suffolk have on employment? For this the only figures available are from the Official Census Returns and they are produced in chart form below.

1   Holman Mss 1720
2   VCH Essex Vol 2 p 463
3   Notes on the Silk Industry - J Corley

Whereas some firms by the 1860's were only employing a few people, firms like Courtaulds, John Hall and Stephen Brown were probably employing 3000 of the 5350 counted in the Census Return for 1861.

Numbers Of Silk Workers Employed And Firms
Essex & Suffolk 1831 - 1891

	Essex	Suffolk	Total	No. of Firms	Av Firm Size
1831*	800	180	980	21	47
1841	1582	874	2456	22	112
1851	2884	1962	4846	21	231
1861*	3200	2150	5350	12	446
1871	2562	1693	4255	11	386
1881	2131	1295	3426	10	342
1891	2604	875	3479	8	435

Source : Official Census Abstracts   * = Estimated Figures

These figures do not reflect the total number of employees in the various firms only those with a specific silk trade occupation.

A further analysis is given of those aged 20+ for the year 1851. Of those aged 20+ working in the silk industry according to registration districts and using this data it is reasonable to suggest the following split to show the total numbers in the Census Districts in the two counties where the industry was to be found.

Area	Number	% of total	Area	Number	% of total
Halstead	1123	39	Sudbury	1453	74
Braintree	1050	36	Haverhill	240	12
Colchester	360	12	Bungay	140	7
Witham	300	10	Lavenham	120	6
West Ham	41	3			
Other	10		Other	9	1
	2884			1962	

From this it is clear that the Halstead, Braintree & Sudbury areas were the main areas of employment.

Places associated with the silk industry

Chapter Four

Where The Industry Was Established

Having looked in general terms as to employment in the two counties just where was the industry to be found? The following index of places has been compiled from information in 19th century Trade Directories and local history sources. Fuller details of the firms and dates of operation are shown in the appendices. The information is as accurate as such sources allow.

Ballingdon

In this hamlet, across the River Stour from Sudbury, Wilson,Casey & Co were trading here in the 1850's.

Billericay

J Machin is mentioned as a silk manufacturer and throwster in Pigot's 1832 directory but not found in any subsequent editions.

Bocking

3 Manufacturers recorded of which the most significant was Samuel Courtauld who started in Bocking in 1826.

Braintree

For some reason, Braintree was favoured by the manufacturers as 12 different firms are recorded as trading from 1809 onwards, of which Samuel Courtauld, Daniel Walters and Warner & Sons became the most important.

Bulmer

J Freestone is recorded in Kellys Directory in 1890 as a silk manufacturer but no earlier references have been found.

Bungay

The Norwich firm of Grout & Co who had a mill operating from 1826 until 1853. The actual mill was in Ditchingham just over the border in Norfolk, but was recorded in the directories under Bungay.

Chelmsford

John Hall of Coggeshall established premises in Hall St in 1855 and these were subsequently taken over by Samuel Courtauld in 1862 and used until about 1890.

Coggeshall

This town was a very important centre of the industry, including several velvet weavers. 13 different names are found for Coggeshall, of which John Hall was the most significant, having a large mill complex in the centre of the town.

Colchester

An early reference to silk weaving here in 1793 by Michael Boyle. In all 6 manufacturers are recorded with Stephen Brown being the largest employer, with a large mill by the River Colne in what is now St Peter's St.

Earls Colne

Samuel Courtauld established premises here in 1882 to supplement the production of the Halstead mills.

Epping

There is an early reference of 1 manufacturer - James Rogers who was in the town for about 5 or 6 years from 1793.

Glemsford

6 different firms mentioned here, starting with Alexander Duff in 1824. The firm of Vanners came to the village in 1871.

Hadleigh - Suffolk

Stephen Brown had a mill here from 1834 until 1853, at one time run jointly with Jon Moy. The mill had a gas works and supplied the town with gas for a period of time.

Halstead

6 firms are mentioned, of which 5 were small one man businesses. The other firm was Samuel Courtauld who started in the town in 1824, having taken over the premises of Beuzeville who had gone bankrupt. The original weatherboarded mill is now an antiques centre.

Hatfield Peveral

South and John Morse were operating as throwsters from 1823 until their bankruptcy in 1827.

Harlow

There is just one entry in a directory for Wm Breavington who operated in the town for about 2 years from 1826.

Haverhill

5 manufacturers worked in the town, with Stephen Walters coming in 1828 and having a presence until about 1880. Vanners came in 1874 and were still operating into the 20th century.

Ipswich

Stephen Brown had premises in Woodbridge Rd in about 1855, but there are little details of this venture. In 1892 Luther Hooper founded the English Silk Weaving Co in Handford Rd and New Cut East and traded here for 10 years.

Kelvedon

John Hall of Coggeshall had a mill here from 1855 until 1862 to supplement his Coggeshall mill. It has been suggested that the mill was actually in Inworth.

Lavenham

Joseph Poulton had a mill in Water St from 1839 until 1854, after which time, it was run by his sister, Mary, until about 1865.

Little Hallingbury

On the Herts/Essex border one of the very first throwing mills was established here in 1720, but later returned to being a corn mill and is now a restaurant.

Maldon

John Luard worked here for about 2 years from 1826 and John Hall had a manufactory in Union Lane from 1855 until 1862, somewhere near where John Sadd established his business.

Mildenhall

Grout & Co worked here for about 2 years from 1826.

Nayland

Stephen Brown had a mill here from 1834 until 1867, at one time run jointly with Jon Moy.

Pebmarsh

Witts & Co with the help of George Courtauld built a mill here in 1799. This was subsequently taken over by E Rodick and this business lasted until 1883.

Saffron Walden

3 manufacturers are found in the town during the period 1815 - 1835 of which Grout, Bayliss were the largest.

Sudbury

Silk manufacturing established in the town from the 1830's although there may have been a home based industry from the 1820's. Like Braintree, Sudbury became an important centre, with 15 manufacturers recorded, of which Stephen Walters & Sons Ltd, and Vanners Silk Weavers are still operating, along with The

Gainsborough Silk Weaving Co Ltd. This latter firm started in 1902, when Reginald Warner acquired the assets of the English Silk Weaving Co of Ipswich

Tiptree

An outpost of John Hall of Coggeshall in Vine Rd, which was taken over by Stephen Brown in about 1862 and worked until 1878 when I believe a brewery, was established on the site.

Waltham Abbey

One of the earliest references in Essex of a mill in about 1720. 5 manufacturers are recorded but silk manufacturing had ceased after 1855.

In all I have identified 100 sites where the industry was to be found, some of which were used by more than one manufacturer. In 1800 there were 4 sites with a maximum of 29 operational in the 1850's . These 100 sites were worked by 70 different firms*, with a maximum of 22 firms working in 1845 and 1855. By 1900 there were just 8 firms working on 12 sites.

It was common in the 19th century for firms to be partnerships - therefore a change of partner created a different firm, but in most cases working from the same site as the old partnership.

The following summary shows how volatile the industry was, with 60% of the sites not lasting more than 10 years.

No. of years	No. of sites
1-5	28
6-10	32
11-15	10
16-20	8
21-25	4
26-30	6
31-39	2
40-50	4
50 +	6

Chapter Five
Working Conditions And Wages

The industry developed at a time when employers gave little thought to the safety and working conditions of their employees. Most employers were proud of the fact that they were giving people employment -and thus keeping them from idleness and the workhouse. It is perhaps difficult today to comprehend the whole ethos of work in 19th century middle and upper class thinking and their fear of the masses rising in revolution if they were not gainfully employed. As our story unfolds from 1798 we must bear in mind that the French Revolution had only recently taken place and as we move into the first ½ of the 19th century there was much discontent in the land and further revolutionary movements in Europe. As one person writing to a local paper put it "work them hard and long and they won't have time to revolt".

Out of this sort of thinking came the 6-day working week, which involved working 12 hours during the day or 10½ hours at night. Because of the nature of most of the work in the silk industry in handling and manipulating silk thread the majority of employees in all trades except weaving were women and children. The Parliamentary enquiry of 1833 into children's employment gives an insight into the numbers of children employed in the silk industry. The following figures relate not only to Essex and Suffolk, but Norfolk as well.

Samuel Courtauld was one of the employers questioned by the parliamentary commissioners who were looking into child employment in factories. In response to their questioning, he stated firmly *"that he was against legislative interference except where strong cases of hardship or wrong could be proven. As far as children employed in silk mills their labour was so light, the mills of necessity clean, dry and airy, that to limit their labours to ten hours per day was wholly unnecessary."*

He did suggest that no children under 10 years of age should be employed and that no one under 17 years of age should work at night or more than 12 hours in any 24. The 19th Century employer felt that his workers should be really grateful for the fact that he gave them work, thus saving them from begging or going into the workhouse.[1]

Children employed in the Silk Industry 1833 Essex, Suffolk & Norfolk

1833	Male	Female	Total
Under 11	12	236	248
11-16 yrs	25	733	758
Total	37	969	1006

Analysis by age and average weekly wage

Age	Number	Wkly wage	decimal
7	4	1/6d	7½p
8	30	1/6d	7½p
9	77	1/9d	8½p
10	125	1/10d	9p
11	148	2/1d	10½p
12	183	2/3½d	11½p
13	152	2/5½d	12¼p
14	122	2/11¼d	14½p
15	128	3/1d	15½p
16	114	3/6¼d	17½p

Source: BPP - Childrens Employment 1833 vol 4

The Parliamentary Report on Child Employment throughout the land shows that even in a relatively harmless industry such as silk, nevertheless it could be dangerous and not a healthy environment in which to work. It is not overstating the fact that many children and young people were affected for the rest of their lives - their bodies malformed from overwork, injury and the ways in which some operations had to be done. Unguarded machinery belts, dust and cramped conditions added to the everpresent dangers to young children in the silk mill. The mills might well have been dry and airy, but with the long working hours there was little chance of anyone benefiting from fresh air and sunshine. Particularly in the winter the mill worker would have left and returned home in the dark. It would have been different if the workers had a diet to give them the strength they needed, but nearly all lived at subsistence level and their food would only have been very basic indeed.

In the early days quite a number of children and young people were recruited from workhouses, particularly in London, and were billeted in cottages near to their work place. John Williams in 1905 wrote *"When young girls were taken on they were given a shilling (5p) which bound them for 12 months. They were subjected to very harsh treatment. If they made too much waste one form of punishment was to wear a brown paper cap called a fool's cap with the waste silk on it all day. The girl I refer to (later his wife) rebelled against wearing the cap and she received a severe beating. After that she left and went to work at the Panfield Lane Mill, but when they found her out she had to repay her shilling"*[2]

There is a report in 1825 in the Essex County Chronicle of the proceedings at the Magistrates Court as a result of 50 girls absconding from Morse's mill in Hatfield Peveral. One girl gave evidence of the fact that she worked from 6am to 7pm, six days a week, with 2 ½ hour breaks for breakfast and dinner. Her wages in her first year were 3s/6d (17½p) per week rising to 4s/-d (20p) in the second year, out of which she paid 3s/6d (17½p) for board and lodging. It is obvious that the Magistrates did not accept that her and her workmates were aggrieved because she was given 7 days-hard labour as a result.

Much later, in 1861, there is a report of silk a worker - Mary Orris- being charged by Mr Bentote, manager of Thomas Kemp and Co in Sudbury, of neglecting her work. The Sudbury magistrates sentenced her to 6 weeks in Bury St Edmunds gaol! The paper commented that this might well have been 6 months, save that her previous good character was taken into account.[3]

Legislation

After the 1833 enquiry attempts were made to regulate working conditions for children and the Factory Act which came into operation in 1836 went some way to help, although in many cases the legislation did not cover silk mills. For instance the Act prohibited children under 9 from working in any mill except silk. Children under 13 were not allowed to work over 10 hours a day and anyone under 18 was not permitted to work at night. Children in mills other than silk mills were restricted to an 8-hour day - 48-hour week - and provision made for some basic education. For some reason silk mill children did not need education. Yet figures given in the report stated that in East Anglia amongst the young people working in the silk trade 81½% could read whilst only 26% could read and write.

In 1844 the working week for women and young persons was to finish at 4.30pm on Saturdays. The minimum age limit was set at 8 and those aged between 8 and 11 were to work a maximum of 7 hours per day. Those aged between 11 and 13 could work a maximum of 10 hours per day. Compulsory education of 3 hours per day was introduced for children up to the age of 11. This was followed in 1847 by the Ten Hours Act, which restricted the working day for women and young persons to 10 hours and for work to finish at 2pm on Saturdays. With passing of the Education Act in 1872 this meant that young children were no longer available for work. Finally in 1874 the working week was reduced to 56 hours.

Wages

Unfortunately adequate information does not exist to enable us to answer the question of what the workers in the silk mills were earning. Figures that are available are generally averages, but nevertheless give an idea of the level of wages in the local industry. Wages were almost static for 20 years from 1830 to 1850 and then rose about 1½% to 2% per annum thereafter. In later years as the industry faced increased competition, elements of the weekly wage were based on piecework rates, which the employers always seem to have been able to adjust to their advantage.

Occasionally one comes across information about wage rates from unexpected sources such was the case when reading the history of Tiptree. In 1859, John Hall established a factory in Factory Lane (Vine Rd). The young spinners were dissatisfied with their pay and Miss Mary South, who was 18 years old, put their plea to the management in verse. Mr Fox was the manager of the factory.

> *Dear Mr Fox don't take this amiss*
> *What sort of pay do you call this,*
> *For the finest silk that can be found*
> *We stand all day for 4 pence a pound.*

They were paid just 4d (less than 2p) for spinning a pound (½kilo) of silk thread. As a result of their plea, the rate was raised to 4½d .[4]

Correspondence in January 1862 in the Essex Standard not only brought to light the poverty of workers, but also a complaint from Stephen Brown of the slanderous nature of the letter. Under the heading "The Season and the Poor" the correspondent, who represented a group dedicated to bringing the plight of the poor to the notice of others wrote as follows:

"There is great distress amongst the poor ... Amongst this class are hundreds who are employed in the factory (an oblique reference to Brown's mill in Colchester) *working 6 days for 4 days pay."*

What the writer was trying to say was that as a result of short time working people were impoverished as they were only paid for 40 hours instead of 60. [5]

The other factor was the lack of any other significant employer, which might have attracted the silk workers .It was not until the end of the 19th century, with the establishment of engineering firms in various localities, that there was any competition for labour amongst the available male workforce.

At Samuel Courtauld's Panfield Lane Mill in about 1825, for turning the throwing engine one man was paid 6/- (30p) whilst another 7/- (35p) and the young lad (12 yrs old) who assisted in this task 2/6d (12½p) per week .[6]

Average Weekly Wages

	1833	1850	1870	1875
7-11 yrs	1/5d	1/5d	no figures	no figures
11-16	2/7d	2/7d	3/5½d	3/10½d
16-21	4/-	4/-	5/4d	6/-
21-26	5/-	5/-	6/9d	7/6d
21-26 men	15/10d	15/10d	21/-	23/-

These rates were about 30% below comparable rates for the same jobs being done in the textile mills of Northern England. However if one compares the agricultural labourers rate in 1875 of 11/- (55p) per week then the men in the local silk mill were comparatively well off. The disparity between men and women is all too apparent, and it is only in very recent times that this disparity has disappeared in manufacturing industries.

Disputes

There are many instances recorded of strikes, but in most cases these were of very short duration. Unfortunately the workforce carried very little clout and one has to remember that there were no organised unions as such. A few leaders emerged to speak up for the workforce, but they had very little practical support. In some cases the workforces found themselves locked out of their place of work.

As an example I have chosen a dispute at Brown & Moy's mill in Colchester in April 1843. The Essex Standard reported that between 200 and 300 women and girls gathered outside the mill gates in protest at being asked to do more work for no more pay.

As a result, 4 women, who were presumably the ringleaders, were brought before the magistrates. The cause of their complaint was that they were in the habit of working 3 reels for 5s (25p) per week, but on Wednesday they were put onto 4 reels for no extra pay. In the past when this had happened they had been paid an extra 1/- (5p) a week. Stephen Brown, one of the owners, pleaded that with the silk industry in depression he felt that the girls were not sufficiently employed and he felt that the extra productivity could be achieved without much more effort.

As the law stood the 4 accused would have been liable to spending 3 months in prison. Stephen Brown said that he was prepared to pay them for work done and then to discharge them. However the chairman of the magistrates recommended they return to work on 3 reels and then reach an understanding with their employers on 4 reel working. It was later reported that an agreement had been reached, although no details are given of the agreed terms of settlement.[7]

The laws of employment, such as existed, worked very much in the employer's favour and there were quite harsh penalties for being absent from work, other than for sickness.

Difficult Times

Life was never easy in the silk industry and short time working was often introduced at short notice. One such occurrence is shown in a notice issued by Samuel Courtauld & Co in December 1854. which is reproduced overleaf.

Dec 8th, 1854

NOTICE

TO OUR
Soft Silk
WEAVERS.

◄●►

THE universal and extreme depression of the Trade, compels us at length to limit the make of all goods but Velvets to Four days' work out of Six.

But feeling much for the Hands whose earnings will be thus reduced by One-third in these dear times, and at the beginning of winter, we mean to make up to them One-third part of the reduction of their earnings.

Thus a weaver whose average earnings have been 15s. a week, will now be restricted to the earning of 10s. But of the 5s. thus reduced, one-third, say 4d, in the 1s., Or 1s. 8d. upon the 5s. will be given to him to help him to bear up under his difficulties.

SAMUEL COURTAULD & Co.

However it is interesting to see how the company was willing to help alleviate the loss of earnings.

After the passing of the Free Trade Act in 1860, which enabled imports from the continent to come in without duty being imposed, the industry as a whole found itself in considerable difficulty. Many firms just went out of business, whilst others scaled down their operations by laying off workers, or shutting down their factories for a time, hoping things would improve.

The following is a précis of an article in the Essex Standard in June 1861 regarding the situation at Braintree.

"In consequence of the distressed condition of most of the weaving population in this town, owing to lack of work, a notice was issued calling a public meeting at the Corn Exchange on Friday evening to take the matter into consideration. About 40 ratepayers and a large number of weavers attended the meeting. The chairman, Rev J Finlayson, said that a superintendent of one firm had told him that he was paying £100 per week less than usual and that it was not likely there would be employment until September. Mr Wheeler (Sanderson & Co) reported that he had 30 hands out of work. William Potter, a weaver, said he never heard of so much distress as at the present time." [8]

Two resolutions were passed at the meeting:

1) That a deputation wait upon the Board of Guardians to respectfully request them to consider affording relief to the families without compelling them to become inmates of the Union Workhouse.

2) That a committee be appointed to obtain information necessary to make a proper representation to the Board of Guardians - to find out how much less wages are being paid than normal and the number of hands out of employ.

The committee found that in 4 firms in the town, 220 employees were out of work. The deputation to the Board of Guardians was not successful and so a subscription fund was raised for contributions and special collections were taken at the various places of worship in the town.[9] Unfortunately I can find no information on how much was raised as it is not mentioned in subsequent editions of the paper. The extent of distress was quite significant effecting over a 1000 people, when dependants are taken into consideration.

Similarly, in Colchester, times were hard when short time working was enforced. There was no guaranteed weekly wage in those days. The workers were paid for the hours they actually worked. As mentioned earlier a correspondent writing to the Essex Standard in January 1862 under the title "The Season and the Poor *"Amongst this class are hundreds who are employed in the factory (a veiled reference to Brown's Silk Factory) working 6 days for 4 days pay"*.[10]

Stephen Brown took exception to the letter as it inferred that he was underpaying his workers and through his solicitor demanded a public apology in the newspaper. The solicitor for Mr James Tabor, who wrote the letter, said "that his client's intentions were to convey that as a result of short time working these workers were impoverished". Mr Brown accepted the apology.

Part of the Braintree Mill built by George Courtauld for Joseph Wilson in 1810

1 History of Courtaulds -Colman Vol1
2 The Story of My Life - John Williams (1905)
3 Essex Standard 24.5.1861
4 Creation of a Village (1977)
5 Essex Standard 17th & 24th January 1862
6 The Story of My Life - John Williams (1905)
7 Essex Standard 7th April 1843
8 Essex Standard 14th June 1861
9 Essex Standard 14th June 1861
10 Essex Standard 17th January 1862

Chapter Six

Domestic Weavers And Outworkers

The tradition of domestic weaving goes back to the cloth trade and in the early days of the silk trade merchants were employing domestic weavers and workers. As the silk manufacturers developed their water powered throwing mills the thrown silk was put out to local weavers. These worked from home and even when larger firms developed and business increased, rather than taking on more employees to cope, outworkers would be used, as these could easily be laid off should demand fall. Domestic weavers were also used to produce small or special orders, which otherwise would be too uneconomical to do in the larger factories.

Weaving was done in their homes or even in garden sheds. In Braintree and in other local towns one can still find evidence of this: - the three storey houses with larger than usual windows on the middle floor where the looms were housed. There were also cottages with a lean to with large windows to let in the light for the weaver. Such properties were built in Rayne Rd - Bocking, St.Michael's Rd, Manor St, East St and South St - Braintree and Melford Rd, Inkerman Terace - Sudbury to name but a few.

Such traditional ways of working are very often viewed with an air of romanticism, such as those homely pictures of "The Weaver at His craft". The reality was long hours of work in cramped conditions and dimly lit rooms together with the tremendous amount of physical effort used to operate the loom which was only partially alleviated by the invention of the flying shuttle.

Courtaulds and Daniel Walters hired out handlooms to domestic weavers, as many could not afford the cost of purchasing one. However if their product was not up to standard the looms were reclaimed. A handloom is easily transportable as it can be taken apart and put onto a cart. It has been known for a weaver, who might be in some sort of trouble, to pack up his loom and be off across country by the next morning.

These outworkers were kept busy when business boomed, but were unemployed when the industry was depressed. Even so the wages were very low and the other members of the family would take on other jobs such as silk drawing or winding. This is borne out by entries in the 1841/1851 Census where father and son are weavers and the mother and daughter take on these other trades.

Other jobs done by outworkers would have included sharpening velvet cutting blades, preparation of selvedge bobbins, bobbin and pirn winding and pattern card cutting.

It would seem in the early days that manufacturers set up small factories in various places, which acted as depots from which skeins of silk were supplied to outworkers and received back the finished material.

Samuel Courtauld did this when he took over Beuzeville's premises in High St, Braintree and until Walters built New Mills in 1856 their weaving was being done by domestic weavers. Vanners too operated a similar scheme in Braintree, Haverhill and Glemsford.

Vavasseur established such a "factory" in Rayne Rd on the corner with Sandpit Lane and others were to be found in the High Street and Martins Yard. Charles Cheeseman opened the last of these factories as late as 1864. He was the son of the manager of Walters in South St, set up in business to produce moire antique and general silks for Messrs Martin & Oliver of London and this enterprise lasted until 1874, using outworkers to do most of the work.

Work done out in this way was carefully monitored by the firm as it would be quite easy for the weaver to use the silk given him to make fabric for some other firm or for himself. A book was kept for each weaver. Some of these are preserved in the Warner Archive, in which was recorded the weight of silk issued on the bobbins for a particular job and when completed the finished fabric was weighed as well as the empty bobbins plus any silk left over. The weaver would then be paid by the yard at a rate according to the type of fabric woven. Deductions would be made if any discrepancy were found between the weight sent out compared to that received back. The firm fixed the rates of pay and so there was very little the weaver could do to compensate for any problems he may have had in producing the fabric.

As the time went on the number of domestic weavers declined, more so from 1860 onwards as the factories could cope with demand themselves. Throughout the 19th century the introduction of power looms put domestic handloom weavers out of work as did the offer of more regular work in one of the factories, with better working conditions. Warner & Sons, were still using domestic weavers for velvet weaving in 1901 at Sudbury. This practice had ceased by the 1920's and all such work was carried out in the factory at Braintree.[1]

1 The History of Silk - Frank Warner (1921) p 308.

Chapter Seven

George Courtauld

It was George Courtauld who was the pioneer of the silk industry in North Essex. It begs the question as to whether without George's involvement at Pebmarsh there would have been a silk industry in this area at all?

The Courtaulds - French Huguenots - came to England in about 1689 and settled in Spitalfields. Samuel Courtauld I - George's father - was by trade a goldsmith, who in 1749 married Louisa Ogier, an accomplished silversmith, whose father was a silk weaver.

George was born in 1761, and in 1775 apprenticed to the silk trade with Peter Merzeau in Osborn St. By 1782, having served his apprenticeship, with the help of £500 left by his father, he set up in Spitalfields as a throwster using horse power to operate the throwing mill. This only lasted 3 years, and George sold the business and paid his first visit to America, and started farming. One gets the impression that he was a somewhat unsettled person, as he returned to Britain in 1788, finding himself a bride, Ruth Minton, whom he married in America on 10th July 1789. He had, by this time, about 600 acres of land in America, but in 1793 or 1794 the family moved back to England. According to son Samuel they had lived a most miserable existence. Already too, it would seem that George and Ruth's relationship was not on the best of terms.

In August 1794 he was working at Peter Nouaille's silk mill near Sevenoaks. It is interesting that Nouaille is accredited with the introduction of crêpe production to England. There is some measure of debate as to whether or not George found out the secret art of crêpe (sometimes spelt crape) from Nouaille, but the production of crêpe was to play a vital role in the development of the Courtauld firm by George's son, Samuel. By 1797, George had lost this job, mainly due to his political views on the French Revolution and republicanism, both there and in America. He then went into the paper making industry in London, but of this enterprise there is very little to be found in the existing family papers.

In 1799, Witts & Co, silk manufacturers of London engaged George, to convert a flourmill at Pebmarsh into a silk throwing mill. He lived at Sudbury and whilst conversion was taking place in a house near the Church in Pebmarsh. In 1801 he and his family moved into the new house, where as manager of the mill he received a salary of £350 per annum, plus a house and 5 acres of land free of rent.

Writing about his work at Pebmarsh he wrote; *"The power of water at the propos'd spot was small, & ye more attention was needful in ye construction of mach^y to perform its offices with little friction. Working hands were to be train'd, & habits of the assiduous ind^y form'd so essential in a manufactory requiring a large number of inferior people. The* *estab^t completed & in a thrifty state, C felt that an ordinary agent might be easily taught to wind up & attend to a machine that he could never have constructed or put together; & yefore, after 9 years attenⁿ, propos'd a perm^t arrang^t to hire ye mills & employ them exclusively for ye prop^{rs} at ye usual prices, or an improv'd & perm^t salary. It was no doubt equally evident to all parties that a less expensive assistant might then proceed with the business, & both proposals were declin'd. In the 10th year of this conⁿ C. left Pebmarsh."* [1]

Never able to stay in one place for long, by 1806 he was looking into the possibility of going into partnership with Joseph Wilson of Milk Street, London. For 3 years correspondence about this venture passed between the two, and finally in March 1809 it was agreed that a former flour mill in Braintree - at the bottom of Chapel Hill - should be acquired and converted for silk production. Wilson purchased the land and property, and George carried out the conversion work, assisted by his son Samuel III. George was then installed as the manager of the mill. Eventually a partnership was formed in September 1814, taking effect from March 1815 for a term of fourteen years, known as Wilson & Courtauld. Under the agreement the premises remained Wilson's property but George Courtauld was given a share in the profits.

In spite of their deal the two partners did not get on very well, and as early as November 1815 disagreements were rife over scales of charges for work done. By January 1816, Wilson refused to supply any more silk to the Braintree mill and production ceased for a while. George retaliated later on by getting supplies of silk from other suppliers. In January 1817, Wilson tried, without success to get the partnership dissolved. However by the end of January 1818 the partnership came to an end, with Wilson retaining the premises, which he then continued to run under his own business of Remington, Wilson & Co. George Courtauld was precluded from running any silk business, other than Pebmarsh, before 1829.

In February 1818, George went to Berkshire to look at the possibility of running a silk mill there, but in the end decided to go back to America. He returned for a short while to England, but went back again to America in 1820, leaving behind his wife, one daughter and Samuel III, who was by this time hard at work on his own silk business.

George died in America on 13th August 1823 - an entrepreneur to the last, but one who for one reason or another never really succeeded in reaching his goal.

However, in spite of this apparent lack of personal success, we must admire his skills and accept that but for George the story told in this book, would have been quite different.

Sources: History of Courtaulds vol1 - Colman: Notes on the Silk Industry - John Corley
1 Courtauld Family Letters (1916)

Chapter Eight

Samuel Courtauld & Courtaulds

Samuel Courtauld III was born in America in 1793, the son of George and Ruth Courtauld. He first became involved in the silk trade in 1807 when he helped his father at Pebmarsh. In 1810 he worked on the setting up of the Braintree mill. By the time he was eighteen he had gained a fair knowledge about the working of a silk mill and that of using waterpower to do throwing. It was then that he left home and went to London, where through the good offices of his uncle, William Taylor, he managed to get a clerk's job.

In 1814 he returned to Braintree to work in his father's silk mill, but this was short-lived, as he became seriously ill in May 1815. On recovery he went to Ireland in the autumn of 1815 to stay with his uncle - John Minton - to recuperate. On his return to Braintree in the summer of 1816 he had decided to go into the silk industry by himself.

In a letter to his sister, Sophia, he wrote of *"setting up a silk manufactory on a very small scale in this vicinity"* [1] (Braintree/Bocking). Premises were acquired in Panfield Lane, Bocking and a horse powered throwing mill built. However there is evidence, that the power was manpower as well, from the reminiscences of an old man who at the age of 12 (in 1825) worked at the Panfield Lane Mill helping to turn the throwing engine. [2] The venture stretched Samuel financially and so in 1817 he approached his cousin - Peter Alfred Taylor I- to join him, and the partnership of Courtauld & Taylor was formed. Pay records suggest that there was employment here for between 90/100 people, mainly women and girls. [3]

The venture was a success and in due course there were thoughts of bigger premises. George I writing to Sophia in Jan 1818 said, *"Sam and Peter have been in treaty for 13 acres of land near Englishes. but could not persuade ye tenant to allow them to put up their building now"* [4]. John English owned land in the vicinity of the Panfield Lane mill.

Samuel writing to his sister Sophia in Jan 1818 : *"Peter Taylor and myself were diligently looking out for a Water Mill; not finding one at present we have resolved to exert ourselves to put our little concern here on a good and permanent footing by Building a Factory for Horse Power large enough to treble our business, but small enough still to be well managed by proxy, when all is elegantly arranged I have promised Peter and myself that this building shall be complete with the moving works - entirely filled with machinery and well organised and fully working in April! Peter says he will give me to next October, but - in April. This little "snug little Mill" will be 60ft. long, 23½ft wide and three stories; weatherboarding beaded edge, painted stone colour with black sashes and Slate Roof."*[4]

Finally a spot of ground was found, at Pound End (South St) Braintree. This was bought for £120 from Mr Grant who lived at "The Limes" in New St.. Writing to his sister Sophia in April 1818, Samuel declared *"The building is as good as finished; my mechinists (sic) are already busy within the walls and I shall redeem my engagement to complete all by May.*[4]

However by 4th July 1819, again in a letter to Sophia, he confided that the Braintree Mill had not come up to expectations, due to external circumstances and that he was seeking to buy Savill's Mill in Bocking. Clearly, from another letter on 7th November 1819 it would seem that the whole venture was heavily in debt owing between £2000/£3000 pounds. In the meantime Savill's Mill on the River Blackwater at the foot of Bocking Church Street had been obtained on a lease and in a letter of 26th November he mentions that they were to move to Bocking Mill.

George Courtauld II writing in a letter of 18th January 1820, notes that Sam has not yet received any money for the sale of the Braintree Mill and that all the machinery had now been moved to Bocking.[4]

Courtauld & Taylor's New Mills had been financed by a loan from George I of £1000, to which was later added a further £800 with George I becoming a sleeping partner in the firm. Also involved was John Newberry, a friend of Samuel Courtauld III who by the time New Mills was sold was owed £800. This total amount of £2600 would equate with Sam's statement in the letter mentioned earlier. The New Mills were sold to Daniel Walters for £900 and this enabled the debt to Newberry to be cleared. George Courtauld I's £1800 was left in the business to be gradually repaid, but attracting 5% interest.

Originally it was hoped that the Bocking Mill would be bought for £2500, but instead it was leased at £100 per annum, thus releasing capital for the conversion work on the mill. Samuel, was , at the time unable to find anyone to come into the partnership with capital. In due course, the site Bocking was developed to include three factories known as Steam Factory, Finishing Factory and Bocking Mills.

At the same time Samuel Courtauld III was in the business of using his knowledge gained both at Pebmarsh and Braintree to convert premises for silk manufacturing. This he had done for a Braintree silk manufacturer named Beuzeville, who had taken over the Townsford Mill in Halstead. However, the operation was too much for Beuzeville's finances and he was bankrupted, and so in due course Samuel took over the mill at Halstead for his own business sometime before 1828.

Land adjoining the mill at Halstead was acquired and in 1832 a Power Loom

Factory opened, equipped with 106 power looms. A second power loom factory was opened in 1836 and yet another in 1842. Meanwhile, back in Bocking, with the expiry of the lease on Savill's Mill, Sam took up the option to buy and at the same time gave up the Panfield Lane factory. He also took on a Broad Silk Warehouse in Braintree, which may have been Beuzeville's property in Factory Yard, High St. This was used as a depot for putting out work to domestic hand loom weavers. Finally, in 1843 he bought the Braintree Mill, which had been converted originally by he and his father, from Remington, Wilson & Co.

The firm of Courtaulds, or to give it is proper name "Samuel Courtauld, Taylors & Courtauld" was now firmly established and growing in size and influence. In July 1846, the employees of the Braintree, Bocking and Halstead factories held a dinner in honour of their employers. The dinner for 1600 people took place in a marquee in a meadow in front of Samuel Courtauld's residence in High Garrett, and a silver medal was struck to celebrate the occasion. At about midday the contingents met and formed a double line on either side of the road, extending for a mile. A loyal address was delivered, read by the secretary, Lister Smith . A fuller account of this event is given in Chapter 13.

Already an office and warehouse had been established in London firstly at Gutter Lane, and then when fire damaged those premises in 1845, this was moved to Carey Lane. By 1849 the firm had established itself as a major manufacturer.

Courtaulds 1850 - 1885

This was a period of sustained growth for the Company, which is quite amazing when one considers the general state of the silk industry after 1860. During the period in Essex 14 silk manufacturers went out of business, representing two thirds of a once thriving industry. At the same time throughout the country many silk manufacturers were forced to close. Incredibly it was during this period that the Courtauld firm expanded rather than contracting. For instance in 1850 the production of crêpe was 28,000 packets, but by 1885 this had risen to almost 50,000.

It was during this time too that Courtaulds lost the original partners, who had brought it into fruition. Firstly Andrew Taylor, who considered by the Courtaulds to be a liability rather than an asset was paid off in 1850. Then in March 1850 Peter Alfred Taylor I died and in April 1861 George Courtauld II died, leaving only Samuel Courtauld III as the sole survivor of the original partnership. He died in March 1881. These changes meant changes in the business, but Samuel Courtauld III still held sway. However, it was the production of crêpe and in particular mourning crêpe that was the keystone to the Company's success. The rise in output together with a general cut in the cost of raw silk, especially after the opening of the Suez Canal increased profits considerably. During the period 1883/5 a profit of £2 per packet was being made giving a 27.8% margin.[5]

The Victorian attitude towards mourning put a great emphasis on women to observe the strict rules of mourning etiquette. Society required a widow to be in mourning for up to 2 years of which a year and a day was in full mourning. During this period at least 3 different sets of clothes, all containing mourning crêpe, would be used. As it was considered unlucky to keep mourning crêpe in a house other than in periods of mourning, once the mourning period had passed all garments had to be disposed of, making way for new purchases as and when the next death in family happened.

With the increased business and good profits finance was put into new premises and facilities. The first was the building of a new three-storey mill at Braintree, completed in 1859, for weaving, winding and throwing. Then in 1865 John Hall - Coggeshall- went out of business and Courtaulds bought his mill in Chelmsford for winding. At Earls Colne a mill was built in 1883 for winding and drawing, which by 1885 was employing over 100 people, mainly women.

Also during the 1880's the main factories in Halstead, Bocking and Braintree were converted from gas lighting to electric, which brought about higher production as the better lighting made it easier to see broken or suspect threads.

The fashion on which the bulk of the business relied changed, which coupled with changes in the economy of the country, suddenly reduced the profitability of the company. No longer was Courtaulds able to rely on an increase in their crêpe trade year by year to give the same returns. By 1895 the profit margins of 1883/5 of £2 per packet, had been eroded to a profit of only £0.10 per packet giving a margin of only 2.3% as the average selling price per packet fell 40% .

1885 - 1900

The economic changes in the country changed the market from the ascendancy of the seller to that of the buyer and the final years of the 19th century were ones of plans for survival. Up until 1885 sales had always increased year by year. However a study of the firm's financial results for the period 1886 - 1894 shows that except for a slight recovery in 1890/1, a decline in sales value of about 50%, from a level of £350,000 in 1885 to just under £175,000 in 1894. No doubt the management of the firm must have wondered whether Samuel Courtauld & Co would still be trading by the year 1900 as they had already seen some of their competitors disappear from the trade.

The Road to Recovery

In 1891 the partnership became a limited liability company and at the same time two new men joined the Board of Directors, Frederick Nettlefold and Henry Browne, both of whom had business experience outside the silk industry. Mr Nettlefold was connected with the family hardware firm, which in the 20th century became Guest, Keen & Nettlefold, and Mr Browne was a stockbroker. Neither of these was completely unknown to the Courtaulds as Mr Nettlefold had married into the Taylor side of the family and Mr Browne had worked with Courtaulds in a professional capacity.

It seems that by 1892 steps were being taken to reduce costs as some hands went onto half time work and there were cuts in expenses and salaries at Head Office. The premises in Hall Street, Chelmsford were finally closed and sold in 1893 and in the same year the new mill at Braintree was shut down for a while.

The company was also fortunate in securing the services of H G Tetley and T P Latham, who between them helped steer the company through this period of change. Not only were there changes in methods, but also changes in types of fabrics as the company sought to lessen its traditional reliance on the production of crêpe.

In November 1894, H G Tetley proposed to the Board of Directors a new weaving facility at Halstead, with 200 additional looms that could produce other silk products. Some were Jacquard looms to weave patterned material. By 1898 Halstead had over 1000 looms in operation.

Modernisation was also an important part of the recovery plan. From archives in the Essex Record Office details are given of a total of 19 steam engines which were in use at Braintree, Bocking, Halstead, Earls Colne and Chelmsford. Of these there were 4 beam engines which were installed at Bocking and Halstead almost 50 years earlier. A decision was made to replace some of the steam engines with gas engines and during the period 1892/95 ten engines were disposed of and by the early part of 1896, 12 gas engines were at work. The company installed its own gas making plants at Braintree, Bocking and Halstead.

All aspects of the firm's operations were examined and each site seems to have been allocated a particular type of work. Bocking, which was the administrative headquarters, looked after the various finishing processes which included the "secret art of crimping". Braintree concentrated on winding and throwing, whilst Halstead and Earls Colne concentrated on warping and weaving. In 1896 the Braintree mill was enlarged to accommodate more winding machines.

Fortunately all these measures brought a turn round in the fortunes of the Company and this is reflected in the financial returns which show a healthy climb in sales by 1900 to £350,000 per annum a figure that had not been attained since 1885. The success in promoting and selling new products, brought about a shortage of throwing capacity and towards the end of the century some of this work was being sub contracted to outside sources.

Sources: History of Courtaulds Vol 1 - Colman 1969; Archives in E R O D/F/3/2—

Pebmarsh Mill built by George Courtauld for Witts & Co in 1799.
Mill demolished in 1901, but mill house remains.

1 Courtauld Family Letters (1916)
2 The Story of My Life - John Williams (1905)
3 ERO D/F/3/2/18
4 Courtauld Family Letters (1916)
5 History of Courtaulds vol 1 p 158

Chapter Nine
Daniel Walters / Warner & Sons

The firm of Daniel Walters came to Braintree in the 1820's. Joseph Walters was a silk weaver at 50 Bow Lane London, the earliest mention being in a directory of 1811. In 1814 his son Daniel joined him, and in Johnstone's 1817 Directory the business is known as Daniel Walters, trading from 8 Hart St, Cripplegate, London. Sometime later Daniel was joined by his brother Stephen and in the London Directory of 1820 was trading as Daniel & Stephen Walters at Wilson St, London. It appears that the Walters worked in their own home for another manufacturer who supplied the raw silk yarn and they were then paid by the yard for the finished cloth.

It was after this date - possibly 1821/2 - the firm moved to Braintree. It is not certain whether Courtauld's Pound End mill was taken over immediately by Walters, as it seems to have been occupied in 1821 by a silk manufacturer called Carter. However a deed exists which proves that in 1822 the mill was owned by William Adams and let to Daniel and Stephen Walters at a rent of £65 per annum.[1]

The mill in Pound End was a Horse Mill for 4 horses with a steam boiler. Stephen subsequently left the partnership in about 1832 to form his own business at Haverhill. This business is operating today in Sudbury.

The firm produced high quality silks and velvets mainly for furnishing and by 1840 developed figured fabrics. This gave a great boost to their business and reputation. In 1849 the firm was awarded a Gold Medal for their silks by the Royal Society of Arts. The business continued to expand so that by the 1850's they were employing about 250, although at this time most of the work was being woven on hand looms in the weavers' own homes.

In 1854 a one-day exhibition was put on at the Braintree Corn Exchange to show the local people what luxurious fabrics were being produced. By 1856, the business was outgrowing the Pound End mill site and an orchard site was purchased on the other side of the road and a mill known as "New Mills" was erected. This enabled much of the outwork to be brought on site and for the first time weavers were working in factory conditions.

Walters received a commission to produce fabrics for the new ballroom at Buckingham Palace in 1856 and thus commenced the link with providing materials for royalty. This type of order must have boosted their prestige which meant that these premises were too small and in 1861 another new mill was built on land bought from Thomas Cheeseman, one time manager of Daniel Walters, on Rifle Hill, which was then in the parish of Black Notley.

The following report appeared in a local paper on 7th August 1861:

OPENING OF MESSRS. DANIEL WALTERS & SONS'
NEW FACTORY

The rapid extension of the trade of this firm, from whose factories are issued some of the most costly and magnificent brocatelles, tissues, satins, damasks, brocaded silks in this country or the world; and in fact every description of silk furniture, has necessitated further provision of factory accommodation; and not withstanding the recent period at which a second factory was erected, a third building has just been raised, and its opening celebrated on Monday last (5th Aug 1861). The new factory is situated in the parish of Black Notley and near the Braintree Water Works and is built on a similar plan to the other factories containing an upper and lower room each 75 feet by 30 feet and a dwelling house adjoining. [2]

At this time the firm had 150 Jacquard looms and employed nearly 300 employees.[3]

More land was acquired in 1869 in South St and the mill on Rifle Hill was taken down and re-erected adjacent to the "New Mills". This building was always known as "The Notley Shop". By 1877 Daniel Walters had two long weaving sheds, one shorter one, together with a dyehouse and workshop. The Pound End Mill was then used merely for storage. The firm also had a warehouse in Newgate Street, London and another mill at Sudbury.[3]

Although sales and production increased, in an endeavour to remain competitive the wages of the weavers were reduced in the late 1860's. A letter circulated to its members by the Furniture Weavers of London gives details of a 14% reduction in wages over the last 2 years, plus a recent demand by the Company to make a yard of cloth 38" instead of the usual 36", which meant extra production for nothing. A deputation of weavers went to the manager to air their grievances, but he refused to see them. As a result on 22nd March 1870 the weavers were locked out from their employment. The letter goes on to ask for subscriptions to help their fellow workmen at Braintree.[4]

Under the direction of works engineer, James Bradbury, 23 power looms had been installed at New Mills by 1875. This departure from traditional handloom weaving was not very well received by the weavers, who perhaps thought that their jobs were in jeopardy, and there are several instances of weavers destroying these "new fangled" machines. Walters at least had the foresight to train the power loom operatives in the art of handloom weaving as well. This new technology meant that fabrics could be woven 63 inches wide, which enabled much larger designs to be woven.

The firm's order books were full and the future seemed bright for both employer and the workforce. Yet in less than 20 years we come across a completely different scenario.

Silk Factory Closes

This headline appeared in the local newspapers of 1894. How then did this successful firm get into financial difficulties? There does not appear to be any one event that caused this but a combination of different things.

In 1886, Daniel Howard Walters died and was succeeded by Lindsey Walters. William Folliott, who had been in partnership with Benjamin Warner, joined the firm in about 1887 as manager and chief designer.

As has already been mentioned in the chapter on Samuel Courtauld this period in the silk industry was one of economic depression, but there seems to have been very little management action to weather this situation. From all accounts Lindsey Walters was more interested in socialising and riding with the hunt, than running the business.

Also there had been a lot of investment in power looms and new technology The working capital was gradually disappearing and by 1891 the firm found itself put in the High Court in London for debts due to some of its creditors. The next few years were difficult, but eventually in 1894 the creditors could stretch credit no further and the firm was forced into liquidation.

Warner & Sons interest

Lindsey Walters took it upon himself to write to Benjamin Warner in 1893 offering to sell New Mills, Braintree. However Benjamin replied on July 20th 1893 to the effect that having studied the proposition, he declined to take the matter any further. However, by September 1894, Warner & Sons agreed to purchase the Braintree operation, including designs, for £78,000.

New Mills closed

Unfortunately this offer came too late in the day to prevent the closure of New Mills in October 1894 as is shown in a quote from the Essex Chronicle on 23rd November 1894.

"The delay in settlement of the affairs of Messrs Walters in the Chancery Court with the subsequent postponement of the re-opening of the Braintree silk factory is unfortunate for the town and particularly for the many weavers who are

waiting for work".

The Essex Chronicle set up a relief fund, for the weavers who had been put out of work and special collections were made in the churches of the town as well. The uncertainty of whether or not Benjamin Warner would be coming to Braintree was not finally concluded until May 1895. In the meantime some Braintree weavers had found employment with Benjamin Warner in London. The Essex Chronicle of 10th May 1895 announced that Benjamin Warner had definitely taken over New Mills at Braintree.

Warner & Sons

Before continuing the story of New Mills, a brief background to the firm of Warner & Sons. The early years are sketchy, but it is known that William Warner, who died in 1712, was a scarlet dyer in the Old Ford area of Stratford. The area was renowned for its production of printed cottons, which required the expert services of such a dyer as William Warner. Five generations on, in 1799 Benjamin Warner was born, and he was a loom harness maker and Jacquard machinist. He had a son, also Benjamin, born in 1828, who was only 11 when his father died. Young Benjamin left school to assist his mother in running the family business, picking up his education at evening classes and finally at the Spitalfields School of Design.

Sometime in the 1860's, Benjamin went into partnership with William Folliott and eventually in 1870, in partnership with Sillett & Ramm established a small silk factory at Old Ford, which eventually moved to bigger premises at Hollybush Gardens, Bethnal Green. Sillett left the partnership in 1874, but Warner & Ramm continued until 1891, when Alfred and Frank Warner, who had been working for the previous firm went into partnership with their father to form Warner & Sons.

The Move to Braintree

In 1895, Warner & Sons still had their premises in Hollybush Gardens in London and it was some time before all production was transferred to Braintree. William Folliott remained as manager of New Mills and Frank Warner (who later became Sir Frank Warner) was made responsible for the production at Braintree. The power looms were set aside as Warners continued the art of hand loom weaving and it was not until 1918 that they were re-introduced. The important aspect was the fact that the local weavers and silk factory employees now had employment once more.

Sources : Weaving and the Warners - Sir Ernest Goodale (1971)
Article by Alec Hunter Essex review vol 62 p 20 (1953)
Notes on the Silk Industry - J Corley

The following broadsheet was published at the time of the changeover in 1895:[5]

The Old Firm

There was once a noted firm,
'Twas a credit to the nation;
Its manufactures were superb,
And commanded admiration.

The creditors required their own,
And sought, by combination,
To secure themselves against their loss,
And resorted to litigation.

And The New

The keys give up, ye vanquished ones,
Ye must succumb to force:
Let a better than yourselves now try,
You have suffered a terrible loss.

So now the said firm has changed hands,
It belongs to Messrs. Warner,
And all success may they obtain,
And keep out of the sad corner.

May success attend their diligence,
Prosperity may they win;
May it prove a stroke of good luck to them,
And the orders come rolling in.

1 Notes on the Silk Industry - J Corley
2 Braintree & Bocking Advertiser 7.8.1861
3 The Silk Industry - Frank Warner p 303
4 Letter F Bragg, Bethnal Green 25.3.1870
5 Essex Review Vol 62 (1953)

Samuel Courtauld's Panfield Lane Mill of 1816
Picture taken in 1926 just prior to demolition

Chapter Ten

John Castle

The reason for including a chapter on John Castle is that it is to him that we are indebted through the medium of his memoirs to get an insight into the silk industry and in particular to what was going on in North Essex. The memoirs are in the Essex Record Office. I intend to put on record some of the more salient points of interest as I feel they portray the problems that people employed in the silk industry faced in the 19th century.

At the age of nine (1829) he went to work with the Coggeshall silk manufacturer - Beckwiths - as a draw boy. This job involved cleaning and separating strands of silk ready for weaving. By chance, one day, a weaver left his loom to go for a drink and John decided to have a go at weaving himself. The foreman sent him off to find the absent weaver. In due course he was given the task of cleaning silk for the foreman and was asked to try his hand at weaving. The foreman found him a talented weaver and immediately gave him a weaving job at 4/- (20p) a week.

In 1837 he found himself out of work, owing to depression in the industry, and had to seek refuge in the parish workhouse. He went to London to find a job, but was offered only one of looking after horses for a silk winder. He walked back to Coggeshall and spent the weekend with his mother before walking back to London to take up his job. Eventually he did get a weaving job, but this did not last long and soon he was out of work once more. He returned to Essex, on hearing of weaving jobs being available at Colchester. He secured employment with Henderson & Co. However, not long after he joined the firm, they decided to shut the Colchester operation and concentrate instead with the factory in Braintree.

John didn't take this situation lying down, he set about organising a deputation to persuade other silk manufacturers to set up business in Colchester to take Henderson's place. He drafted a petition and gained approval from the Mayor, his deputy and the town's two Members of Parliament as well as representatives from local banks. Writing to the Essex Standard he then sought the support of the general public. The letter was published in the 28th December 1849 edition of that paper. The first men to go to London early in 1850, returned, having had no luck whatsoever and then it was suggested that on their second planned visit John Castle should be one of the number.

It was then that previous work in London came to John's aid, as when they came to Friday Street, John remembered a firm he used to visit - Campbell, Harrison & Lloyd. Having found the premises they went and saw Mr Campbell, who asked them to return later. The rest of the day was spent visiting other manufacturers, one of which was Vanners of Spital Square. Next day they received a favourable response from Mr Campbell. The party returned to Colchester much heartened by their success.

In due course someone from Campbells came to Colchester, where the premises were inspected and talks held with the Mayor. All that was needed was for a foreman to be appointed who would run Campbell, Harrison & Lloyd's firm at Colchester. John fully expected to be given this job, but the post was offered to someone else. Never one to give up, he resolved to move to Braintree to find work. However, some days later he heard that he had in fact been appointed as foreman, a position he held until his death in 1875. He was well respected not only be his employers but also the employees.

By 1861 he was at the forefront of setting up the Colchester Co-operative Society. It was he who took the initiative, dealing with opposition from other sections of the business community. His tenacity to a cause, which he had already shown in getting work for silk workers, won the day and the new Society set up in business on 2nd August 1861.

Courtauld's Bocking Mill
Building to the left is the original built
by Samuel Courtauld III

Chapter Eleven

A Coggeshall Weavers' Story

This is the story of Mr & Mrs Charles Musk who were the last of the Coggeshall velvet weavers. Their story would never have been recorded had not the Essex County Standard sent a reporter to interview them in 1911. The full text may be found in the copy of the paper for 18th July 1911. The reason for the interview was the fact that Mr & Mrs Musk were weaving velvet for the coronation of King George V.

Charles Musk was born at Coggeshall in 1845. His father and mother, grandfather and an uncle were all weavers. At the age of ten, Charles was apprenticed to John Hall at the Orchard Mills. The weaving was done on the first storey, where skylights provided good light for the 50 looms at work there. Most of the weavers were apprentices and youths. Downstairs, in the same building, young children were involved in throwsting and winding. These children, in 1855, started as ½ timers at the age of 8, spending the other ½ day at school.

Having served a 3-year apprenticeship, Charles worked at home with his father, mother and sister on one of the 4 handlooms they had in the house. In 1871 he married. His wife had been apprenticed as a velvet weaver to Westmacott, in Church St, Coggeshall. At this time there was plenty of work and there were several master weavers in the town. Not all had factories, but instead supplied materials to the weavers, who carried on their industry in their own homes. The majority of weavers preferred to work in this way, but some masters insisted on the work being done at their own premises. If weavers went into the factory they had to pay 6d a week to the master for the loom to stand in the factory. This levy helped towards the master's overheads.

With the resumption of peace between France and Germany following the end of the Franco-German War in 1870, the English market was hit by cheap imports of velvet from the continent. This velvet was sold at 2/- (10p) per yard, which was less than the weaver in this country was paid for weaving the cloth, let alone the cost of the materials as well. The result of this was that many smaller master weavers went out of business. Charles and his wife left Coggeshall for Yarmouth, where Mr Musk was foreman and his wife, a weaver, in a silk crêpe factory. After nine years they returned to Coggeshall to again take up velvet weaving. However by this time, (late 1880's), there were only about 20 looms at work in the town, mainly working for Bailey, Fox & Co.

Wages

As mentioned previously, weavers were paid by the yard of cloth produced.

Whilst serving his apprenticeship, Charles was paid just ½ of the going rate of 2/6d (12½p) per yard. This meant his weekly wage would have been about 9/- (45p). Even as a qualified weaver, at the end of the apprenticeship, he would only be earning about 15/- (75p) a week. In 1911, at the time of the interview, Mr & Mrs Musk were each being paid just 18/- (90p) a week.

There is an example of Mr Musk's velvet that can be seen in the Coggeshall Museum at the Coggeshall Heritage Centre.

Chapter Twelve

Other Manufacturers

The industry was organised in different ways with large firms carrying out all the different processes, whereas others specialised. Although calling themselves manufacturers, some were in fact, warehouses which received their supplies from outworkers working at home, and sold on to either other manufacturers or their own manufacturing centres elsewhere in the country. Certainly at the beginning of the 19th century the local firms were supplying products for Spitalfields until they themselves developed their own markets. These were in the minority and the majority of firms continued to supply the London market as well as some of the larger local concerns.

Courtaulds, Walters and Warners have already been dealt with. What follows is a brief look of some of the other manufacturers.

Witts & Co - Pebmarsh 1799-1809 E Rodick 1809-1883

The flourmill in Mill Lane was bought in about 1798 and a new throwing mill built on the site by George Courtauld and run by him until he joined up with Joseph Wilson in 1809. Quite why Pebmarsh was chosen is a mystery, as it was and still is a quiet remote rural village. One thought is that the village was midway between the silk centres of London and Norwich and labour was more plentiful and cheap in the country.

Daughter, Sophia wrote years later of her father *"building a factory, dwelling house and cottages for workpeople, and turning a wilderness into a scene of tasteful comfort and extended usefulness"* [1]

Whilst the conversion was taking place, George and his family lived in a house near the Church.[2]

The building was a three-storey mill, and had a twenty feet diameter water wheel, which in a Parliamentary Return for 1838 was rated at 8 hp. In 1821, Rodicks installed a 5 hp horizontal steam engine by Peel & Williams using a Symington & Atterton boiler on the first floor.[3] This may seem odd at first sight, but the first floor would have been level with the top of the bank, and the ground floor would have housed the water wheel. The shafting and gearing would have been on the first floor, making it much easier to harness the power of the steam engine. It is not clear whether the steam power was supplementary, or merely a standby should the water supply give up. The small river called the Peb was harnessed to work the mill, by building a high bank about 12 feet high which formed a lake for the water, which was then fed onto the wheel by a sluice. This is clearly shown on the 1897 O.S 25" plan. The present owner has reduced the height of the bank, but it still looks impressive, and there still remains a lake in the garden, which was the northern end of the original construction.

The coming of the silk mill, which in 1836 was employing 95 workers (44 of whom were under 18 years of age), had a profound effect on the economy and social development of the village. It gave, to the female population the ability to become a highly skilled workforce. The mill in 1836 must have taken in workers from other places, as the 1841 Census Returns for Pebmarsh show a total of only 53 people from the village employed, of which 51 were female. Of these, 36 were under 20 yrs of age, 8 of whom were under 10, and 2 who were only 7 years old! By 1861, 96 people from the village were employed, 93 of who were female. This represented a large proportion of the eligible female working population of the village. The business was taken over by E Rodick and then E Rodick and Son, finally ceasing in 1883.

In 1893 the property was purchased by George Courtauld, grandson of the builder, but owing to the dilapidated state of the mill this building was demolished in 1900.

Archibald Rodick died in 1934 and left a sum of £100 to be distributed by the Vicar to old women in the village of Pebmarsh being old mill hands, who have resided in the village for ten years. At that time there were still four parishioners who were former mill hands.[4]

Grout Bayliss -Bocking & Saffron Walden 1800- 1832

Joseph Grout was a loom harness maker in business in Bocking Church Street in 1800. Then in 1801 he formed a partnership known as Grout Bayliss & Co in Norwich.[5] This firm became the largest silk manufacturer in East Anglia, with offices in Foster Lane, London. By 1826 it was employing over 3500 persons in Norfolk & Suffolk, as well as handloom weavers in Bocking, Braintree, Saffron Walden and Sible Hedingham.[6] The firm is recorded in the trade directories for Bocking from 1826-1832, and it seems likely that this was a warehouse for distributing work to and from home workers. I have not been able to establish exactly where the premises in Bocking were, but there is evidence to suggest that it was near to the junction of Church Lane with Bradford Street.

Remington,Wilson & Co - Braintree 1810 - 1843

Joseph Wilson of Milk Street,Cheapside,London traded as Remington,Wilson & Co and in 1809 acquired a former flour mill (Megs Mill) in Chapel Hill, Braintree. He engaged George and Samuel Courtauld to do the necessary conversion for silk production and the cut from the River Brain was enlarged to provide the additional waterpower. George was appointed as mill manager and in 1814 a partnership known as Wilson & Courtauld was formed. Wilson still retained the ownership of the property, but was George was entitled to a share in the profits. Owing to differences between the two the partnership was dissolved in 1818, and the business continued to run under the name of Remington, Wilson & Co until the premises were sold in 1843 to Samuel Courtauld. (Joseph Wilson was highly regarded in the City of London, a member of the Weaver's Company and in 1839 was Lord Mayor of London.)

Sawyer & Hall 1818-1828
John Hall 1828- 1865 Coggeshall

Sawyer & Hall were established in Coventry, and in 1818 set up a branch at Coggeshall employing 150 people. John Hall could see the potential of the Coggeshall business and in about 1828 the partnership was dissolved and John Hall then ran his own company. He established a throwing mill at the Abbey Mill and a factory at The Gravel, where he made ribbons and velvets. He was advised and helped by Samuel Courtauld in this project . In 1834 he decided to build a steam mill across the road from the Gravel in West Street. Building commenced in 1837 and it was opened for business in 1839 and known as the Orchard Mill. The main mill building, built in red brick, as opposed to weatherboarding, had 3 floors covering an area 180ft x 45ft (165m x 41m) plus an Engine House 47ft x 23 ft (43m x 21m) with a chimney 110 ft (100.6m) tall.[7]

Quite early on he gave employment to over 400 people plus the services of handloom weavers and by mid 1850's he opened depots at Tiptree and Maldon.[8] In the P.O Directory of 1855 there were depots at Hall St Chelmsford and Inworth.

According to the Victoria County History in the 1860's the total number of people in his employ was 700 which made him the second largest silk manufacturer, surpassed only by Samuel Courtauld's businesses at Braintree, Bocking & Halstead.[9] This figure is borne out by the record in the 1861 Census of some 660 employees. It is no wonder that Hall had to expand his operation out of Coggeshall, because there was just not enough local labour available in the town. There is also evidence that many local parents were opposed to their girls being employed in the industry because of poor pay and working conditions.

Sometime towards the end of the 1860's the business ceased and the Orchard Mill and the mill at Tiptree were taken over by the firm of Stephen Brown in Colchester whilst the premises in Chelmsford were bought by Courtaulds.

The Orchard Mills were subsequently bought in 1894 by John King, the seedsman and an engraving of the premises was included in the 1895 and 1896 catalogues. The engraving probably contains a good bit of artist's licence but it docs give an idea of what Orchard Mills would have looked like. Much of the site was destroyed by fire in the 1920's and is now part of a housing development.

Stephen Brown 1826 - 1869
Colchester, Hadleigh, Nayland & Ipswich

Stephen Brown born in 1797 came from a family of millers. Nothing is known of his reasons for moving into the silk industry, but he must have had capital to embark on building, in 1826, a purpose built steam powered throwing mill in Colchester. The site, which occupied an area of 230 ft x 190 ft (210.5m x 174m), was adjacent to the River Colne in what is now known as St Peter's St. The main mill building 81 ft x 39ft (74m x 36m) was built in red brick on 4 floors. There was also a smaller mill and reel room which were 39ft 6ins x 14ft 6ins (36m x 13.3m) and 33ft 6ins x 15ft (30.7m x 13.7m) respectively both 4 floors high. Finally there was a single storey winding shed 102ft x 51ft 6ins (93.3m x 47m) and an engine house complete with a 90ft (82.3m) chimney.

Upwards of 400 women were employed here, which increased to 600 when a night shift was in place. With the opening of other mills, Stephen Brown was employing well over 1100 people, second only to Samuel Courtauld in size of operation.

In 1834, in partnership with Jon Moy, mills were set up at Hadleigh and Nayland in Suffolk, where the mills had a gas works, which not only supplied gas lighting for the mill but also supplied gas to the locality. Sometime in the 1850's a mill was opened in Woodbridge Rd, Ipswich employing about 300 but no mention is made in the local directories anywhere after about 1855. However in October 1871 it was reported in the Essex Standard that the Ipswich factory had infringed the Factory Act so we must assume this was operating until about 1879 when the Colchester factory closed. After John Hall's business closed in 1864/5, Brown took over Hall's premises at Coggeshall and Tiptree. The mill at Nayland closed in 1867 and the one in Hadleigh in 1869. After Stephen Brown's death in 1869 the business was taken over by R Durant, who had other businesses in the Eastern Counties, and eventually closed the business in about 1877. A former manager then rented the Colchester premises and tried to continue the business but this failed in about 1879. After Durant's death his executors put all the properties up for sale in 1886. The Eagle Brewery used the premises in Colchester and the buildings stood until pulled down for re-development in the 1960's.

Stephen Walters & Son 1828 to Present Day
Haverhill, Sudbury

Stephen was brother to Daniel Walters who ran his business in Braintree, which was sold to Warners. The firm is still in business in Sudbury with, I believe, the 9th generation of the Walters family at the helm and as such is the oldest silk manufacturer in the country .

In 1828 Stephen, having left the business in Braintree bought a former tan yard in Haverhill Hamlet, which in those days was in the county of Essex, and built a silk factory. Built of brick to the first floor, the upper floors are timber framed, rendered on the outside and plastered internally. Each floor had room for 16 looms per floor. In 1840 it was said that there were 70 looms at Haverhill. By 1874 the firm had opened premises in Sudbury, and when in the 1880's it experienced a downturn in business the Haverhill premises were sold to John Atterton. John had an engineering business, which still trades on the site as Atterton & Ellis. However the firm did return to Haverhill in the 1890's and continued there until the 1930's.

Stephen Walters & Co became a limited company in 1899, when it also acquired the business of Messrs Kipling & Dennier, and established the headquarters of the company in Sudbury, where it still trades today.

Vanners Silk Weavers

This firm has its roots in Spitalfields, having been founded in the late 1820's by John Vanner (1800 -1866). The firm had premises in Braintree from 1855 until about 1862, which could well have been a warehouse to distribute and collect work from domestic weavers. It is thought that they were in Pound End on the opposite side to New Mills, but I have been unable to trace the exact site. Premises in Colne Valley Rd, Haverhill were constructed in 1865 and in 1874 a warehouse built at Glemsford. The brick built 3 storied building in Haverhill could accommodate 60 looms. With a head office in London, local managers were employed to oversee the production. With competition from power looms at the end of the 19th century, James Vanner sold the firm to George and Frank Fennell of Haverhill. The Company then became Vanners and Fennell Bros Ltd and establishing itself in Gregory Street and Weavers Lane, Sudbury.

1 Courtauld Family Letters (1916)
2 History of Pebmarsh (1946)
3 "The Mill House, Pebmarsh" Peter Bushell & Sara Van Loock c 1990)
4 The History of Pebmarsh (1946)
5 Notes on the Silk Industry - John Corley
6 History of Courtaulds Vol 1 Page 63
7 ERO D/DC27/685
8 The History of Coggeshall 1700-1914 WEA
9 VCH Vol 2 pp 462/9

Sam Watson weaving at Warner & Sons

Chapter Thirteen

The Impact Of The Industry On The Locality

Today established industries in Essex and Suffolk make an impact on the day to day life of the community. In times past the industries which established themselves in the two counties made much more of an impact to the development and culture of a town or village. One has only to cast one's mind back 30 or 40 years to see how employers such as Warners, Courtaulds, Vanners and Walters put their blueprint on a community.

In a previous chapter we saw how employment was provided. In this chapter we look at the impact of the industry on social activities, welfare and the economy. Although wages were low the owners of the firms, for whatever reason, made recompense by putting some of their wealth back into the community.

Social Activity

As a result of the long hours worked, particularly in the first half of the 19th century, finishing at 7pm at night or late Saturday Afternoon, left very little time for social activities or recreation, even if one could find the energy! However there was a great sense of loyalty to the employers, and there was gratitude by the employees for employment. There were times when disgruntled employees took industrial action, but these actions never lasted for long.

What follows gives an idea of the types of activities that were arranged by different firms.

Courtaulds

The Courtaulds are noted for their provision of welfare and other facilities, not only to their employees but also the wider community.

The first example however is something that the employees of Courtaulds did for their employers on the 26th June 1846 when the employees of Courtaulds held a dinner in honour of their employers. Brief mention has already been made in Chapter 8, that is worth repeating in more detail now. The proceedings were published in a 40-page booklet, the following of which is précis taken from that booklet.

"This week we have to record the proceedings of a festival of a novel character, inasmuch as it is totally unconnected with party political feelings but was given by the numerous hands in the silk and crêpe factories of Messrs S Courtauld, Taylors and Courtauld in the three towns of Bocking, Braintree and Halstead - a spontaneous display of goodwill and respect of the employed to their employers.

The spot selected was the parklike meadow of 12 acres in front of S Courtauld Esq's residence in High Garrett. A spacious marquee was erected for the dinner capable of containing 2000 persons; a number of refreshment booths supplied provisions to the spectators who also attended. The tradesmen in Halstead and nearly the whole of those in Bocking and Braintree, as a mark of respect closed their shops and made the day a general holiday.

The Braintree and Bocking employees began to muster at The Hyde (Braintree Market Place) between nine and ten o'clock. Thus marshalled they marched off escorted by the Bocking Band. In all there were about 700 in the procession bearing a variety of tasteful and appropriate silks banners and in order according to their trade. They passed along Pound End (South St), High Street and down into Bocking. Near the Six Bells (Bradford St/Church Lane corner) 5 carriages carrying members of the firm and their friends and made their way along Church Lane and Church Street, Bocking joined them.

Meanwhile the 800 strong Halstead contingent accompanied by the Halstead Band and with appropriate banners and in order of trade was also making its way to Folly House and the two groups came together soon after 12 o'clock. Both processions merged four abreast and made one procession about 1 mile in length and thus made their way into the meadow, with the carriages bringing up the rear.

At one time it is believed that there were five or six thousand people in the field and it was estimated that during the whole day dome eight or nine thousand people attended the proceedings. (This number was equivalent to almost 75% of total population of the three towns at that time). Two o'clock came and the 1500 employees filed into the marquee for dinner. A top table for the principal guests was arranged along the width followed by two tables lengthwise filled with tradesmen and other visitors from Bocking, Braintree and Halstead. After dinner speeches and responses were made, although because of the throng the customary toasts were dispensed with.

Towards the end of the proceedings the workpeople presented their banners and the assembled company left the tables. Towards evening the throng gathered for a display of fireworks, which commenced at half past nine, arranged by Mr Darby of London and by half past ten people were making their way home. Thus peaceably and orderly closed the proceedings of a day, which appeared to give unalloyed delight to all, engaged in it, and certainly forms an epoch in the history of the manufacturers of Essex."

The start of that last sentence may seem odd, but we must remember that the 1840's was a turbulent period not only in Great Britain but Europe as well with the upsurge of republican movements on the Continent and the Chartist movement in our own country. Large gatherings of people made the authorities very afraid that activists would turn them into a riot and therefore it was a credit to all that the day was peaceful and orderly .

50 years later, in 1896, a dinner was held to commemorate this event, to which were invited not only current employees but also those who had participated in that celebration in 1846.

Walters & Sons

An exhibition was held in 1854 in Braintree Corn Exchange to show to the local people what kind of silk weaving the firm was doing. The event was recorded in the Essex Standard:

> *"The specimens of their workmanship, consisting of rich, brocaded tissues and other damasks were much admired, many visitors not previously aware that such costly goods were manufactured in Braintree"*

It was also an opportunity for a celebration dinner, for 200 workpeople plus several local tradesmen. The dinner was provided by Mr William Joyce, landlord of the Bull Inn (Braintree Market Place) and the proceedings presided over by the manager at Walters - George Cheeseman. As was common with such events toasts were proposed, one being by Mr Lebow, a weaver, who proposed a toast to the health of Messrs Walters & Son.

In 1861 to commemorate the opening of their new buildings in South St a special day of celebrations was held, which was reported widely in the local paper:

> *"At one o'clock the work people, numbering from 250 to 300 persons met at the Old factories whence headed by the Braintree Brass Band they walked in procession through the town to the new factory bearing a large number of banners etc. of their own workmanship and various elevated bouquets. The interior of the new building was gaily and tastefully decorated with flowers,evergreens, banners etc, and an excellent dinner provided by Mr.Cook, of the Black Lion Inn, Braintree. To this bountiful spread the whole operatives were liberally invited. Mr George Cheeseman occupied the Chair; Mr George Chapman filling the vice chair. On the removal of the cloth the usual loyal and complimentary toasts were given, followed by the toast of the evening 'The health of Messrs. D Walters & sons and prosperity to their trade.' which was proposed in an appropriate speech by the chairman and received with three times*

three upstanding ... In the evening A Ball took place dancing being kept up with spirit until 12 o'clock. The festivities of the day were unmarred."

Outings/Treats

Paid holidays were not provided, but instead employers would arrange, at their own expense outings and treats.

The first outings were probably to the Great Exhibition of 1851, when employers the length and breadth of the country arranged for employees to attend using the recently developed railway system.

Walters & Sons

Sometimes the outings were extended to include employee's family and friends as was the case for the Walters and Sons outing on Monday 2nd August 1858 to Harwich. Accompanied by a band, 600 people marched to Braintree station at 8am for the outing On arrival at Harwich, some took the boat to either Ipswich or Walton on the Naze. Having thus enjoyed their day out they made the return journey to Braintree, which unfortunately took longer than anticipated. The train having reached Marks Tey (having left Colchester at about 9pm) stalled on the gradient, and in spite of several attempts to move, had to await the arrival of an engine from Colchester to assist. This was successful and eventually the train arrived back in Braintree a little after 1am! However, whilst at Marks Tey, 3 or 4 people had alighted from the train and gone for a walk, only to find on their return that the train had gone without them![1]

In 1862 an excursion was arranged to take employees of Walters & Sons to London to attend the International Exhibition, where examples of the firms silks were on show. A special train was hired and party of about 250 marched to the station accompanied by the band of the 12th Essex Rifle Volunteers.

On the 4th September 1863, the annual treat for Walters' employees was held locally. At 12 midday about 300 employees assembled at the factory and accompanied by the Foresters' Band, marched through the town to Mr Perry's meadow in Bocking. During the afternoon they played cricket, football, quoits, "kiss in the ring" and took part in dancing. Then at 5pm the assembled company marched back to Braintree Corn Exchange where they partook of an excellent tea supplied by Mr S Piggin of the Wheatsheaf Inn. The chair was taken by the manager - Mr George Cheeseman. The Corn Exchange was tastefully decorated for the occasion and many splendid specimens of their workmanship were exhibited. Having eaten, the tables were cleared, dancing re-commenced, interspersed with occasional speeches.[2]

There was a factory excursion by special train to Walton on the Naze for all employees in June 1868. Once again a band accompanied the party. It was also recorded that as well as footing the cost of the excursion each employee was given a small gratuity to spend during the day.

Stephen Brown

Mention is made in July 1861 of upwards of 300 silk girls employed by Stephen Brown going to Birch Hall, the home of Mr & Mrs Charles Round and this event seems to have been an annual event at least until 1868. Not only were there sports and substantial tea with fresh fruit, but an address by a visiting clergyman as well, thus giving "refreshment to body and soul". Time and again one comes across concern by employers for their employees moral welfare such as this. The girls would go in a procession of vans (as many as 13) loaned for the day by various tradesmen, including the Great Eastern Railway, headed by the band of the Colchester Volunteers.

On the 4th September 1869, 600 employees from Colchester and Ipswich went to Harwich, the employees from Colchester going by train and those from Ipswich going down the River Orwell by boat.

Campbell, Harrison & Lloyd

In July 1863,[3] under the supervision of John Castle, employees had an excursion to Harwich, where they went boating and sailing or strolled along the beach. Later in the afternoon they took tea at the Alma Coffee House, before departing for home.

Welfare

Although, as we have already seen, working conditions were harsh, employers such as the Courtaulds were concerned for the welfare their workforce. Work and welfare were after all part of the ethos of the Victorian industrialist. For instance in Gosfield and High Garrett, where members of the Courtauld family lived, schools were built from funds supplied by the family for the benefit of the community. Coffee and Reading Rooms were established in these villages and the building at Gosfield (opposite the Kings Head) still has the sign "Coffee and reading Rooms" painted on the wall. The Courtaulds, who were supporters of the Nonconformist movement and put money into the establishment of the Nonconformist based British & Foreign schools in the locality. To encourage their employees to improve their education and to get them away from spending what little free time they had in the local alehouse, Evening Schools were organised and "Mechanics Institutes" were set up in both Braintree and Halstead. Both these Institutes had a Reading Room, with a good supply of books and newspapers and in 1852 a Reading Room was set up in Bocking as well.

It is interesting to find that in December 1850, Mrs Courtauld started a Nursery for mothers who worked at the Halstead factory in order to encourage married women to continue in employment. Children and babies were cared for from 6am until 6pm for which a charge of 1s/6d per week was made. Nursing mothers were able to feed their babies during the day at 8.15am, 11am, 1.15pm and 4pm. The older children were given a meal of boiled rice and treacle for dinner. The Nursery was closed in September 1853, as it was not used a lot, women preferring to have their babies and toddlers looked after by other members of the family instead. I can find no reference to similar facilities at either Bocking or Braintree, but this may be due to the fact that the major portion of surviving company archives from the early days are from the Halstead mill. From the family letters it would seem that the female members of the Courtauld family were quite heavily involved in seeing to the provision of welfare for the female workers.

Housing

The labour force of the silk manufactories was not just drawn from the immediate local area. Certainly the records from Courtaulds Halstead Mill show quite a number of employees coming from outlying villages. In the early days, as has been mentioned, young girls were taken on from workhouses in London. In Pebmarsh in 1799 George Courtauld provided housing for such employees. Cottages were built in Mill Hill, Braintree for employees of Remington, Wilson & Co in 1809. John Hall of Coggeshall also had cottages for his employees, who may have been weavers working from home. As the century progressed more houses were built, certainly by the larger concerns, and very often they had a distinctive "company style". The type of housing provided ranged from terraced houses to semi- detached or even detached dependent on a person's status within the company. Distinctive cottages were built by Courtaulds in Bocking, Gosfield and Halstead (which can still be seen today) for their senior and skilled workers. In common with most houses built by the firm quite prominently placed are the initials of the particular Courtauld who had them built and a date.

The Co-Operative Movement

For some reason weavers had a great sense of community - they lived and worked together. There was mutual concern, and although I have no proof locally, certainly in Spitalfields the formation of Friendly Societies for the well being of working people came from weavers and others connected with the silk industry. It is then of no surprise to find that weavers and silk men were behind the formation of Co-operative Societies, having as their pedigree the Rochdale Pioneers (1844), in both Braintree and Colchester. At Colchester it was John Castle who was the driving force behind the setting up of the Colchester & East Essex Society in 1861. Sometime after this discussions took place in Braintree about forming a local Co-operative Society. These were held at the home of John

Cowell and also at the George Inn, where the landlord was William Shead. Both men were master weavers. Having made a decision to proceed it was necessary to raise some capital and asking interested people to contribute 1/- (5p) per week did this. The treasurer for the fund was Joseph Flude, a foreman at Daniel Walters & Sons, who when the Society was officially formed in May 1864 was the first president. The first store was set up in Pound End (South St) in the centre of the weaving community.

The Economy

As a flourishing industry there was an impact on the local economy with wages being spent with the shopkeepers and other businesses. With nearly 100 sites where the industry was carried on this in itself created business for builders, carpenters, brickmakers, timber suppliers. When Walters built the mills in South Street, Braintree, the cast iron supports for the ceilings and floors were cast at the nearby Rayne Foundry and it seems likely that Courtauld, John Hall and Stephen Brown all made use of local foundries to supply various ironwork for their premises.

The introduction of steam powered mills required the special skills of boilermakers and the purchase of steam engines and boilers. This in turn meant supplies of coal and coke for the furnaces, which created work for carters, coal merchants and the railway. Raw materials and finished goods would have to be taken to and from the various premises and this too would affect local businesses.

In those communities where the silk industry was a major employer, the wealth and prosperity of the community rose and fell with that of the silk industry.

Mention has already been made of short time working and closures and certainly when silk factories closed large numbers of people were effected. In September 1879 when the factory, previously owned by Stephen Brown, closed 130 hands were reported out of work. 48 had applied to be retrained as needleworkers under a scheme devised by well meaning people in the town such as the Round's from Birch Hall. But as the writer to the paper said it was employment not charity that these people needed. I put this in as an early example of retraining for other skills, which is found today in various government backed retraining schemes. In the paper for 11th October 1879 mention is made of the fact that some women had in fact been re-deployed in other places in the town.

1 Essex Standard 6th August 1858
2 Essex Standard 11th September 1863
3 Essex Standard 24th July 1863

Chapter Fourteen

Conclusion

The story so far has concentrated on the industry in the 19th century to give an indication of just how important silk was to the communities of North Essex and South Suffolk.

Although employment in the silk trade has diminished, particularly from the 1970's, nevertheless the firms operating today have an affinity with their Victorian predecessors. After all the basic principles are the same, although modern technology has replaced many of the old methods. There is however one exception to this generalisation and that is The Humphries Weaving Co Ltd, who still produce silk fabric on 19th century handlooms.

At the present time, the local silk industry is thriving, albeit on a much smaller scale and the following snapshots of the industry endeavour to give an idea of the importance of these companies to the silk industry of the United Kingdom. Indeed, Sudbury is now considered to be the silk weaving capital of the UK.

The Humphries Weaving Company
Braintree & Castle Hedingham

Richard Humphries was the last textile designer for Jacquard weaving to be trained at Warner & Co in Braintree. When that company closed, Richard acquired various looms and other equipment from the New Mills site and set up business in 1972, firstly in Sudbury and then established the De Vere Mills at Castle Hedingham. As the business expanded these premises became very cramped and so a new site was sought. In 1985 the Braintree District Council took on the restoration of New Mills, Braintree and in 1990 the Humphries Weaving Company moved into part of the restored complex, taking with them looms that 20 years before had worked there, and established The Working Silk Museum. This enabled not only the business to expand but also the opportunity for members of the public to see at first hand how silk is prepared and woven. The space released at Hedingham by the move to Braintree was used to provide a dye house and the installation of silk throwing machinery as well, which made the company more self-sufficient. The company however is not a museum piece but a commercially run business producing high quality hand woven silk fabrics and hand cut velvets. Richard carries on the traditions of Walters and Warners in producing high quality fabric. His firm was called upon to supply fabric for the refurbishment at Windsor Castle following the fire. Other commissions have included supplying fabric for Hampton Court, Audley End and the Csar's Palace in St Petersburg.

Vanners Silk Weavers
Gregory Street Sudbury

The main business has been the production of woven silks for tie and scarf manufacturers and the company is part of the Silk Industries Group. However, the company is moving into weaving silk for clothing other than ties and for furnishings.

In 1968 Vanners Silk Weavers merged with David Evans & Co of Crayford, Kent and worked together until 1980 when bought out by Seker International. Seker were in due course taken over by Stoddard Holdings plc - carpet manufacturers. Stoddard found it difficult to merge these specialist firms into their operations and as a result in 1988 some senior managers of Vanners & Evans made an offer of a management buy out. An agreement was reached and the new company came into being in February 1989, since when it has gone from strength to strength. In 1995 the company Silk Industries plc was floated and since then it has acquired Biddle, Sawyer & Co - silk fabric importers and silk printer Adamley Textiles of Macclesfield. In recent years a great deal of investment has been made in the latest technology such as electronic Jacquard looms.

The group has mill shops at Crayford and Sudbury where silk products can be purchased and there is a very interesting museum at Crayford , which is well worth a visit , particularly as it concentrates on silk printing rather than weaving.

Gainsborough Weaving Co
Sudbury

Established in Sudbury in 1902 by Reginald Warner, who had previously worked for the English Silk Weaving Co in Ipswich. The firm produces quality fabrics for specialist markets which includes materials produced under Royal Warrant and employs about 30. It has its own preparatory section for bobbin winding, much of which is still done by traditional methods and its own fully equipped dye house. The bulk of the weaving is done on first generation Hattersley box looms with Jacquards using the 400's pattern cards but these are now being phased out. Alongside these are a group of Dornier looms in conjunction with Bonas Jacquards. More recently a Data Weave loom, linked to a Bonas Jacquard loom which gives added scope to translate a wide variety of designs and qualities from our archival collection. This new venture has been made possible by the introduction of Computer Aided Design facilities in the design department.

Stephen Walters & Co
Sudbury

David Walters, the present Managing Director, is preceded by 8 generations of the Walters family who have run the business since the 18th century and as such is the oldest silk manufacturing company in the UK. The production in Sudbury is mainly centred on making silk fabric to be made into silk ties. An associate company - David Walters Fabrics - at Acton - produces silk fabric for curtains and upholstery whilst another factory at Glemsford spins and dyes the yarn for the looms at Sudbury and Acton. The company gives employment to about 250 people and its products are sold worldwide, with 75% of production going for export.

Appendix I

Essex & Suffolk Silk Manufacturers 1800-1900

Location	Manufacturer	1800	1810	1820	1830	1840	1850	1860	1870	1880	1890	1900
Ballingdon	Wilson,Casey						**					
Billericay	J Machin				**							
Bocking	Wm Newman	*****	****									
Bocking	S Courtauld			*****	******	******	******	******	******	******	******	****
Bocking	Grout Bayliss	*****	*****	*****								
Braintree	Remington Wilson		*****	*****	**							
Braintree	S Courtauld			*****	******	******	******	******	******	******	******	****
Braintree	Walters			*****	******	******	******	******	******	****		
Braintree	Beuzeville			***								
Braintree	Henderson Arundel					*****	*****	**				
Braintree	Vavasseur					*****	*****	**				
Braintree	Sanderson,Reid					*****	**					
Braintree	Vanners					*****	**					
Braintree	Martin & Oliver								***			
Braintree	Martin & Thomas								****			
Braintree	Duhoit									*******		
Braintree	Warner & Sons									*****	****	
Bulmer	J Freestone									**		
Bungay	Grout & Co			*****	*****	****						
Chelmsford	John Hall						*****					
Chelmsford	Samuel Courtauld						*****	******	*****			
Coggeshall	Richard Smith		*****									
Coggeshall	John Hall		*****	*****	*****	*****	**					
Coggeshall	Joseph Lawrence		****									
Coggeshall	Wm Beckwith		****									
Coggeshall	Benjamin Goodson					*****	*****	**				
Coggeshall	Thos Westmacott					*****	*****	**				
Coggeshall	Samuel Clark					**						
Coggeshall	Louis Gachet					**						
Coggeshall	Thomas Brooks						******					
Coggeshall	J Ashton						***					
Coggeshall	Benjamin Wilson						***					
Coggeshall	Stephen Brown							******				
Coggeshall	Sparling & Co							**				
Colchester	Michael Boyle	****										
Colchester	Stephen Brown			*****	*****	*****	*****	*****	***			
Colchester	W Williment				***							
Colchester	Jn Moy				***							
Colchester	Wm Comber				**							
Colchester	Brown & Moy					****						
Colchester	Henderson, Arundel					***						
Colchester	Campbell/Harrison						*****	*****	**			
Earls Colne	Samuel Courtauld									*****	*****	**
Epping	James Rogers	*										
Glemsford	Alexander Duff			*****	*****	****						
Glemsford	Joseph Foote						*****	*****				
Glemsford	Vanners								*****	*****	*****	**
Glemsford	Heaton & Co								****			
Glemsford	Foot,Burton										**	

		1800	1810	1820	1830	1840	1850	1860	1870	1880	1890	1900
Glemsford	Kipling, Dennier											**
Hadleigh	Brown & Moy				*****							
Hadleigh	Stephen Brown					*****						
Halstead	John Davies			***								
Halstead	Jones & Foster			****								
Halstead	Samuel Courtauld				***							
Halstead	Paul Horace				**							
Halstead	Joseph Ash					*						
Halstead	Elijah Finch									*		
Hatfield Pev	South & John Morse			***								
Harlow	Wm Breavington			**								
Haverhill	Stephen Walters			******************************								
Haverhill	Thos Kemp & Son						********************					
Haverhill	Joseph Foote								***			
Haverhill	Vanners									*********************		
Haverhill	Kipling & Co										******	
Ipswich	Stephen Brown						************					
Ipswich	English Silk W Co										*****	
Kelvedon	John Hall						*****					
Lavenham	Joseph Poulton					********						
Lavenham	Mary Poulton						*****					
Maldon	John Luard			**								
Maldon	John Hall							****				
Mildenhall	Grout & Co			**								
Nayland	Brown & Moy				*****							
Nayland	Stephen Brown					***********						
Pebmarsh	Witts & Co/Rodick	**										
Saffron Walden	Grout Bayliss			*********								
Saffron Walden	J Archer			**								
Saffron Walden	Peter Bedford				****							
Sudbury	Alexander Duff			******								
Sudbury	Witts & Co			**								
Sudbury	John Hill			****								
Sudbury	James Hill					******						
Sudbury	Joseph Foote					****						
Sudbury	John Edmunds					****						
Sudbury	Duff & Peacock					****						
Sudbury	Keith & Co						*					
Sudbury	Stephen Walters									********************		
Sudbury	Kipling Pain									*************		
Sudbury	Daniel Walters									************		
Sudbury	Kipling Dennier									*****		
Sudbury	Thos Kemp									************		
Sudbury	Wm Jones										****	
Sudbury	H W Towell										*****	
Sudbury	Gainsborough S W Co											***
Tiptree	John Hall						*****					
Tiptree	Stephen Brown							*********				
Waltham Abbey	Carr & Dobson			*****								
Waltham Abbey	Forsyth & Lincoln			********************								
Waltham Abbey	John Woolrich		**********************									
Waltham Abbey	John Carr			****								
Waltham Abbey	J Buttress				*****							

Appendix II

Fabric Types & Processes

The type of fabric is determined by its use. For instance garment fabrics are much lighter weight than those used for furnishings. The types that follow are but a sample of the many available.

Garment Fabrics

Taffeta - a very rich, fairly stiff material - used for dance and evening- wear. As the wearer moves it produces an attractive rustle.

Satin - a material with a lovely lustre of which Duchesse is perhaps the most well-known, being used for wedding dresses and evening wear.

Crêpe de chine - feels soft and warm - alternative weft threads are tightly twisted in opposite directions.

Chiffon - a plain weave sheer, lightweight fabric.

English Gum Twill / Foulard - made using long twist yarns for scarves and ties.

Furnishing Fabrics

Damask - usually made in a single colour depending for its effect on the contrast on the effect of light on warp and weft weaves.

Brocatelle - A much heavier fabric than damask, with the figure in the warp satin and the ground in the weft. Behind the silk warp and weft is a linen weft, which gives fullness and an embossed quality to the pattern.

Brocade - This had its origins in the 18th century, when handloom weavers sprays of flowers were woven on a figured damask ground. They used small shuttles which did not necessarily go the full width of the cloth. Nowadays the weft goes the full width of the cloth. The pattern appears as raised figurework.

Dual purpose Fabric

Velvet - the richest of all fabrics with the unique light reflecting property of its pile. This pile is created by the introduction of threads, which stand up at right angles. The loops formed by these threads are cut, making them into tufts. The weaving of velvet is a very specialist skill. It can be woven plain or figured.

The Processes

Reeling

This process is carried out where the cocoons are produced. The cocoons are put into warm water to enable the gum to soften and the ends of the threads to detach. A number of these threads are brought together and wound onto large square reels. This creates a skein of silk and the skeins are made up into a "book" which weighs about 10lbs. The book was put into a straw bag to make bales, which are then shipped from the country of origin - mainly China nowadays but in the 19th century, several other countries as well.

Washing

This is done to clean off any dirt and also to make the thread more pliable for the next process.

Winding

The raw silk is wound off the skeins onto bobbins and cleaned by being drawn on a drawing engine onto a second set of bobbins ready for throwing.

Throwing or Throwsting

The term comes from old English meaning "to twist" which gives a clue to the process involved. Other fibres are spun for weaving, silk however is thrown. The process involves using two sets of bobbins running at differential speed, the differential determining the number of twists per inch put into the yarn any thing from 10 to 70+. The throwing of silk by the throwster is to produce a final thread made up of a given number of individual silk threads, doubled together to create a given thickness or denier. A number of silk threads are twisted together at a given number of twists per inch and then turned with a similar number of threads which have been prepared with a reverse twist. The highly twisted yarns were used for silk crêpe manufacture. The denier of silk is the weight in grams of 9000 metres of yarn.

Degumming

The natural gum is boiled off, which makes the thread softer.

Dyeing

Silk may either be dyed before or after weaving, depending on whether a patterned or one colour cloth is required. Printing using, either a handblock, silk screen or roller may pattern plain cloth. The dyeing process is important as it determines the shade and colour of the finished woven silk. The dyer in times past would keep a book in which to record how particular shades of colour were obtained so that they could be repeated.

Warping

The threads, which run lengthways in the cloth are called the warp threads. The bobbins wound with thread are placed on a creel and drawn onto the warping mill and then transferred to a warp roll in readiness for them to be put onto (entered in) the loom, each thread parallel with its neighbour and properly tensioned.

Twisting and Warp Knotting

To make up a warp of sufficient length some means has to be used to join the threads together. From the new roll of warp threads, individual ends are twisted onto the remaining warp threads already in the loom harness, known as the thrum. The joining process was done by a Twister, using a finger and thumb action, with the application of butter to act as a lubricant during the process and as a hardening agent at the point of the twist. Nowadays, a knotting machine is used. This slowly tracks across the two sets of warp threads, which are prepared in a tight position, one group superimposed above the other in readiness for the machine to select the two individual threads to be knotted together, with the ends neatly cropped.

Spooling/Pirning

The preparation of the pirns for use in the shuttle to produce the weft threads - those that go across the cloth.

Entering the warp threads

To enable a loom to produce a fabric, warp threads need to be lifted in a regulated manner, to create the opening or "shed", through which the weft threads are conveyed by the shuttle or rapier. The lifting of the warp threads is through the action of a set of heddles or a harness. This is composed of loops or eyelets (made of glass or brass) equal to the number of warp threads through which through which the warp threads are inserted with the aid of a threading hook. This is called entering.

Creating a pattern

The designer is one of the most important employees, as without him the weaver would not have designs to work to. The choice of designs came either from customer's ideas or as the industry progressed from catalogues of designs produced by the manufacturers themselves.

Jacquard Cards

For elaborate designs, punched Jacquard cards are used. Joseph Jacquard, a Frenchman, invented the card system, in 1804. The design is transferred onto point paper, which is squared paper similar to that one would use for graphs. The cards are punched with a hole to correspond with the position of a coloured square on the point paper. Cards are cut for a particular colour, so that if there is more than one colour another card is required. The position of the holes in the cards enables the loom to create the pattern. The cards are laced together to form an endless band The cards pass through a Jacquard machine that is situated on top of the loom. When the machine finds a hole in the card a needle passes through the and connects with a hook which lifts the necessary warp threads to produce the pattern.

Weaving

Handloom weaving is highly skilled, involving an enormous number of hand and feet movements to operate the loom. First the treadle is pressed down to lift selected warp threads, then the reed moved back to make a space, known as "shed", for the weft thread to be passed across by the shuttle. The reed is moved forward to pack the threads together. This process continues until the amount of cloth required has been woven.

Books for further reading

Courtaulds - An Economic and Social History
- D C Coleman OUP 1969 3 Vols.
Vol 1 for the 19th Century
A History of Courtaulds C H Ward-Jackson (1941)

The Silk Industry
- Frank Warner Drane 1921

Shire Albums:
No 194 The Silk Industry
- Sarah Bush
No 135 Textile Printing
- Hazel Clark

William Folliott - Spitalfield Designer
(The Working Silk Museum, Braintree)

The Last Handloom Weavers
(Macclesfield Museum Trust)

A Choice of Design

Weaving and the Warners
- Sir E Goodale (1971)

Victoria County History of Essex
Vol 2 pp 462 - 469

Places to visit

The Working Silk Museum
- New Mills, Braintree Essex
01376 - 553393

Working Silk Museum
Now closed down

The Humphries Weaving Co Ltd
- the only commercial handloom weavers in the UK.
See work being done on authentic 19th century handlooms.
The shop sells gifts made from silk woven on those looms.

World of Silk
- Museum & Shop
David Evans & Company Bourne Rd Crayford Kent
01322 - 559401
Silk printing division of Silk Industries plc

Vanners Silk Shop
- Gregory St Sudbury Suffolk
01787 - 372396
Silk weaving division of Silk Industries plc

The Silk Museum
- Macclesfield Cheshire
The Heritage Centre
01625 - 613210

Paradise Mill
- Macclesfield   Cheshire
Park Lane
06125 - 618228

Whitchurch Silk Mill
- Whitchurch Hants
01256 - 892065
Water powered mill

Braintree District Museum
Manor Street Braintree
01376-325266

Display and resource centre
on local textile industry

Index

Free Trade Act 1860, 18
Freestone   J, 9

G
Gainsborough Silk Weaving Co Ltd The, 12, 56
Glemsford, 6, 10, 45
Gosfield, 51
Great Eastern Railway, 51
Grout & Co, 9
Grout Bayliss & Co, 11, 42

H
Hadleigh (Suffolk), 10, 44
Hall John, 7, 9, 11, 12, 28, 39, 43, 44, 52
Halstead, 7, 10,26, 28, 47, 48, 51, 52
Harlow, 10
Harwich, 50, 51
Hatfield Peveral, 10, 14
Haverhill, 7, 10, 31
Haverhill Hamlet, 45
Henderson & Co, 37
High Garrett, 27, 48, 51
Hooper Luther. See English Silk Weaving Co
Hours of work, 13, 15
Hugenots, 23
Humphries Richard, 55
Humphries Weaving Co . The, 55

I
Ipswich, 11, 12, 44, 50, 51, 56

K
Kelvedon, 11
Kemp and Co, 15
Kersey, 1
Kipling & Dennier, 45

L
Latham T P, 29
Lavenham, 1,7,11
Little Hallingbury, 5,11
London, 2, 3, 4, 6, 23, 24, 25, 27, 31, 32, 34, 37, 41, 42, 43, 50
Long Melford, 1
Luard John, 11

M

Machin J, 9
Maldon, 11, 43
Marks Tey, 50
Martin & Oliver, 22
Merzeau Peter, 23
Mildenhall, 11
Minton John, 25
Morant, 5
Morse South & John, 10, 14
Moy Jon, 10, 11, 44
Musk Charles, 39, 40

N

Nayland, 11, 44
Nettlefold Frederick, 28, 29
New Mills, 31, 32, 33, 34, 55
Newberry John, 4, 26
Newman William, 5
Norwich, 2, 41, 42
Notley Shop, 32
Nouaille Peter, 23

O

Ogbourne, 5

P

Panfield Lane, 6
Panfield Lane Mill, 6, 16, 25
Parliamentary Enquiry 1833 Children's employment, 13, 14
Pebmarsh, 5, 11, 23, 25, 41, 42, 52
Poulton
    John, 11
    Mary, 11
Pound End, 26

R

Rayne Foundry, 53
Remington, Wilson & Co, 5, 24, 27, 42, 52
Rivers
    Blackwater, 6, 26
    Brain, 6, 42
    Colne, 6, 10, 44
    Orwell, 51